Living the Christian Life

Also by Ben Campbell Johnson

Speaking of God:
Evangelism as Initial Spiritual Guidance

Discerning God's Will

An Evangelism Primer:
Practical Principles for Congregations

Pastoral Spirituality: A Focus for Ministry

Rethinking Evangelism: A Theological Approach

To Pray God's Will: Continuing the Journey

To Will God's Will: Beginning the Journey

LIVING THE CHRISTIAN LIFE

A Guide
to Reformed Spirituality

Robert H. Ramey, Jr.
Ben Campbell Johnson

Westminster/John Knox Press
Louisville, Kentucky

Scripture quotations from the New Revised Standard Version of the Bible are copyright © 1989 by the Division of Christian Education of the National Council of the Churches of Christ in the U.S.A., and are used by permission.

Book design by Gene Harris

First edition

Published by Westminster/John Knox Press
Louisville, Kentucky

This book is printed on acid-free paper that meets the American National Standards Institute Z39.48 standard. ♾

PRINTED IN THE UNITED STATES OF AMERICA

9 8 7 6 5 4 3 2 1

Library of Congress Cataloging-in-Publication Data

Ramey, Robert H. (Robert Homer)
   Living the Christian life : a guide to reformed spirituality /
Robert H. Ramey, Jr., Ben Campbell Johnson.
      p.   cm.
   Includes bibliographical references.
   ISBN 0-664-25286-9

   1. Christian life—Presbyterian authors.   2. Spirituality—
Presbyterian Church.   3. Presbyterian Church—Doctrines.
I. Johnson, Ben Campbell.   II. Title.
BV4501.2.R325 1992
248.4′85137—dc20   91-32250

To

Gail and Nan:

Our best friends,

our loving critics,

and

our partners in marriage!

Contents

Responsibilities of the Christian Life

Preface

We are concerned about our church's decline in member-ship and influence over the last twenty-five years, and we are persuaded there will be no reversal of present trends, nor pervasive revitalization, apart from a deep renewal of the Spirit in personal and corporate life. Such a revitalization can come, we believe, through the recovery of an authentic Reformed spirituality. We share John A. Mackay's affirmation of Reformed piety:

> For deep in the heart of Calvinism, and in Presbyterianism, in its truest and most classical form, resides a profound piety, that is, a passionate experience of God linked to a profound devotion to God. . . . It is piety in this sense that provides the requisite dynamic for the conduct of church affairs and the application of Christianity to life in all its fullness.[1]

In this book we explore the roots of this piety and suggest practices that will enable Presbyterians, and others sharing the Reformed heritage, to understand and live more fully the Christian life.

We have examined Reformed spirituality also because of the nagging conviction that the Presbyterian Church (U.S.A.) has neglected its roots. Furthermore, both of us have nurtured a long-standing interest in spirituality, and we began this task with the anticipation that our lives would be enriched and challenged by the research. In this hope we have not been disappointed.

Since we teach in a Presbyterian seminary, we have desired that our students' Christianity be formed by their spiritual tradition. However, available instructional resources have lacked the dual emphasis on theology and practice, both of which are important.

In our research we have received primary guidance from John Calvin (*Institutes of the Christian Religion*), John H. Leith (*John Calvin's Doctrine of the Christian Life*), Ronald S. Wallace (*Calvin's Doctrine of the Christian Life*), Karl Barth (*Church Dogmatics* and *Prayer*), and the *Book of Confessions* and the *Book of Order* of the Presbyterian Church (U.S.A.). In addition, we have consulted a number of other sources to round out our understanding of Reformed spirituality. (See Bibliography.) We offer this book neither as a historical survey nor as a comprehensive theological analysis of Reformed spirituality but as a theological and practical guide to the subject.

We believe that a true Reformed spirituality will lead all of us into a deeper life with God. To relate such insight to contemporary experience we have begun each chapter with a situation in the church today. We proceed to explore the doctrine involved with references to time-honored sources of the tradition, and we conclude with practical suggestions for appropriating these insights for our lives. In the final chapter we have focused on reforming the church so that it may be spiritually generative, and we have recommended various strategies to help leaders in the congregation become reformers.

In the appendices we have provided lesson plans and exercises, which will assist in the teaching of the text in study groups, congregations, or seminary classes. The exercises offer ways to apply the insights in the book. Our intent is to satisfy a student's intellectual curiosity, while providing practical directives aimed at deepening the experience of God.

Finally, we hope Presbyterians will manifest in their lives the dedication called for on the Calvin crest, which depicts a hand reaching down to a flaming heart and offering it in devotion to God. The words inscribed around the crest are: "My heart I give thee, Lord, eagerly and sincerely!"

We are indebted to C. Benton Kline, Jr., Walter Brueggemann, Douglas W. Hix, Glenn Bucher, and numerous others who have read the text and made helpful suggestions. Harold Twiss provided able editorial assistance for which we are grateful.

Robert H. Ramey, Jr.

Ben Campbell Johnson

Living the Christian Life

THE FOUNDATION
OF THE
CHRISTIAN LIFE

1

To Be
a Christian

Peter and Mary Simpson stand with a dozen other prospective members at the baptismal font of First Presbyterian Church in Middletown, U.S.A. Earlier in the service of worship they heard the promises of God in the call to confession. Dr. Sarah Makemie, pastor of First Church, had said, "The proof of God's amazing love is this: while we were sinners Christ died for us. Because we have faith in him, we dare with confidence to approach God." These words echoed in their minds as they were presented by an elder for membership in the church.

The elder, speaking on behalf of the session, presented all twelve candidates by name and said: "These persons have studied God's Word and have learned the belief and practice of the church. They were baptized as infants and now desire to profess their faith publicly. They want to assume greater responsibility in the life of the church and its mission in the world."

Dr. Makemie continued, "We rejoice that you now desire to declare your faith and to share with us in our common ministry."

Quoting Matthew 5:14–16, she addressed the group. "You are the light of the world. A city built on a hill cannot be hid. No one after lighting a lamp puts it under the bushel basket, but on the lampstand, and it gives light to all in the house. In the same way, let your light shine before others, so that they may see your good works and give glory to your Father in heaven."

Then Pastor Makemie said, "Now, as you publicly declare

your faith, I ask you to reject sin, to profess your faith in Christ Jesus, and to confess the faith of the church, the faith in which you were baptized.

"Do you renounce evil, and its power in the world, which defies God's righteousness and love?"

Each person in the group responded: "I renounce them."

"Do you renounce the ways of sin that separate you from the love of God?"

"I renounce them."

"Do you turn to Jesus Christ and accept him as your Lord and Savior?"

"I do."

"Do you intend to be Christ's faithful disciple, obeying his word, and showing his love to your life's end?"

"I do."

"Do you promise to participate actively and responsibly in the worship of the church, Christ's Body?"

"I do."

Turning to include the congregation the pastor continued, "With the whole church let us confess our faith. Do you believe in God the Father?"

Each person responded, "I believe in God the Father almighty, creator of heaven and earth."

"Do you believe in Jesus Christ, the Son of God?"

"I believe in Jesus Christ as the only son our Lord who was conceived by the Holy Spirit and born of the Virgin Mary. He suffered under Pontius Pilate, was crucified, dead, and was buried. He descended to the dead. On the third day he arose again. He ascended into heaven and is seated at the right hand of the Father. He will come again to judge the living and the dead."

"Do you believe in God the Holy Spirit?" asked the pastor.

"I believe in the Holy Spirit, the holy catholic church, the communion of saints, the forgiveness of sins, the resurrection of the body, the life everlasting. Amen."[1]

One may wonder exactly what the confession of faith meant to Peter and Mary. Perhaps the people in the congregation understood the service as one thing, the minister another, and all those present likely would stand in sharp contrast to Calvin's Geneva congregation. What does it mean to profess your faith publicly or renew your profession?

A wide range of possible motivations exists for Peter and

Mary: a desire to improve their social standing in the community; a hope to provide Christian activities for their children; a genuine interest in God awakened by the failure of individualism and materialism to make their lives meaningful; the need for comfort and hope following the death of a loved one; a desire to dedicate themselves to the glory of God.

Which motive compelled Peter and Mary, we cannot say with certainty. We hope they have an image of God in their minds and commitment in their hearts that coincide with those called for in the church and written in the Bible. Yet if we should interview this couple, or others within the church, we wonder how they would answer the question of why they joined the church.

David Steele, a Presbyterian minister, has defended the Peter and Mary Simpsons of our church, claiming they are not fuzzy or foggy in their faith—neither are they tepid, wishy-washy Christians. He suggests that as a whole Presbyterians do not fit the stereotype of ill-formed, marginally committed persons described by many. Rather, they are persons who have lived through the 1960s with a loyalty to the church when 85 percent of their generation are no longer involved. Each Sunday they, as a family, are perhaps the only ones on their block pulling out of the driveway and heading to church. They go because they believe in the church and know what the church stands for.

Steele maintains that Mr. and Mrs. Average Presbyterian may possibly be faulted for not using religious language. "If you ask them about their faith, they can verbalize it quite well. . . . Since they do not thrust their religious language into every conversation, they are people of Matthew 6 who are careful not to practice their piety before other people."[2]

Perhaps the Presbyterians whom David Steele knows do understand their faith and have been maturely formed by it, but scores of persons we meet within the church do not measure up to this standard. A recent report to the General Assembly of the Presbyterian Church (U.S.A.) more nearly expresses our findings: "Christians are hungry for renewal in their lives of faith. They want to know what it means to be alive and mature in Christian faith and they are calling for guidance and support in developing the disciplines and practices by which their faith may be nurtured and sustained, experienced and expressed."[3] The report goes on to say that this hunger may appear among other Christians but is especially characteristic of those in mainline churches, including the Presbyterian Church (U.S.A.), whose members "all too often feel that their own churches are unclear and inadequately helpful in these concerns."[4]

The Substance of Christian Commitment

Those who now come into the church, as well as those who have been involved for some time, will benefit from examining the meaning of Christian commitment and the Christian life. Being a Christian can be summed up in the following statements:

1. To be a Christian is to be awakened to the goodness and mercy of God through the proclamation of the gospel of Jesus Christ.

2. To be a Christian is to recognize that you are a sinner before God and need God's grace in order to be saved from the power and guilt of sin.

3. To be a Christian is to place your faith in Jesus Christ as Lord and Savior and to repent of sin.

4. To be a Christian is to intend to be Christ's faithful disciple, obeying his word and showing his love to your life's end.

5. To be a Christian is to belong to the church, Christ's Body, and to participate actively and responsibly in its worship and mission.

What do these five affirmations mean? What real difference does it make if we claim to be Christians?

1. A Christian has been known, loved by God, redeemed in Jesus Christ, and called into community before the foundation of the world. Being a Christian does not begin with us, with our need, our hunger for meaning, nor with our fear of death but with the gracious love of God. God took the initiative to call the world into being and to make us in the divine image. The idea of our existence always belonged to the sovereign God.

Because of this amazing love, God not only made and sustains us but chose to come into our midst in the person of Jesus Christ. Jesus is Emmanuel, "God with us," God in a form that we can see, hear, and respond to. The life, ministry, death, and resurrection of Jesus Christ was God's way of bringing us back into fellowship with the divine plan and purpose.

After his departure into the divine presence, Jesus sent the

Holy Spirit into the lives of his faithful followers creating his Body on earth. The church re-presents Christ; it is his "earthly form of existence." Since coming into the world the Holy Spirit has been giving life to the church and calling men and women to faith in Christ and participation in his community.

A Declaration of Faith (1977) gives expression to this truth in these words:

> We testify that today this same Holy Spirit
>   makes us able to respond in faith to the gospel
>   and leads us into the Christian community.
> The Spirit brings us out of death into life,
>   out of separation into fellowship.
> The Spirit makes us aware of our sinfulness and need,
>   moves us to abandon our old ways of life,
>   persuades us to trust in Christ and adopt his way.
> In all these things we are responsible for our decisions.
> But after we have trusted and repented
>   we recognize that the Spirit enabled us to hear and act.[5]

Peter and Mary Simpson stood before the congregation in Middletown that Sunday morning not only because they were facing some existential crisis in their lives but also because the sovereign God had demonstrated in Christ a compassionate love for them and because they had been acted upon by God's grace through the Holy Spirit. Whether they knew or understood these realities or not does not nullify God's gracious love and sovereign action.

2. A Christian has recognized that he or she is a sinner before God and needs God's grace to be saved from the power and guilt of sin. According to John H. Leith, "The central unity in Calvin's theology is the explication of the personal relationship between God and humankind."[6] Unfortunately, this relationship does not begin with a positive desire for God, but often with a repugnance for God. According to Calvin, the human plight consists in our having been created in the divine image, but this high estate has been dissipated by sin. Adam's rebellion against God affected all his posterity. To acknowledge that we are sinners means admitting to something desperately wrong in our lives, both in motivation and orientation.

When Peter and Mary say they are sinners, they are confessing in part that they have been born into a sinful world, into a world in which much human behavior violates the will of God. Following the example set by their forebear Adam, they have suspected the integrity of God, turned from God, have set themselves at the center of their world, and have looked to the world rather than to God to fulfill their deepest hungers. All of us participate in a world in which everyone is a sinner—no one escapes this charge.

This tragic situation for all persons is further complicated by the fact that we cannot in our own strength find the way back to God. Our rationality, though not destroyed, has been so weakened that it cannot reach God. Also, the will has been so enslaved by sin that it does not "aspire after the good."[7] Since we have no natural desire for God, and even if we did we could not return to God, our situation is, to say the least, desperate.

To be a Christian, therefore, means to acknowledge that nothing we can do will restore us to a right relationship with God—not our good intentions, good works, moral character, nor even our faith. To acknowledge the futility of all our efforts prepares our hearts to receive from God what we cannot do for ourselves. Could it be that those joining First Church had come to the awareness of their utter helplessness and were being drawn to Christ by God's Spirit?

3. A Christian has faith in Jesus Christ as Lord and Savior. God did not leave us alone in the futility, misery, and alienation of our broken relationship with our Creator. God chose "Israel for the sake of all, and now all are, in Christ, loved and, through Christ, saved, freed, forgiven, rescued, and redeemed by God for no other reason than God's sheer gracious goodness."[8] This gracious God has taken the initiative to cross the chasm which separated us from God. In Jesus Christ, God chose us and created a way that we can be received into fellowship. This generous act depends not upon our goodness nor upon our merit but upon God's mercy. In traditional language, God "justifies" us sinners. Although we do not deserve it, God has declared us righteous and has ascribed to us the righteousness of Christ.

In the history of religion, two ways to God have struggled for domination, the way of works and the way of grace. By works we mean whatever humans can do in their own efforts to gain a relationship with God; by grace we mean the free, unmerited offer of forgiveness in Christ apart from human effort. Ephesians 2:8-9 gives a clear witness: "For by grace you have been saved through faith, and this is not your own doing; it is the gift of God—not the result of works, so that no one may boast."

So our right relationship with God comes through Christ and Christ alone. And yet the offer must be received, if we are to enter into a new relationship with God. How do we respond to this incredible gift of grace? By faith, which the Holy Spirit creates. We accept God's gift, receive it, and rest upon Christ alone.[9] We turn from sin and turn to Christ and his way of righteousness.

Peter and Mary, along with the other members, placed their faith in Jesus Christ to overcome their alienation. God's grace through faith restored them to a right relationship. Their faith included beliefs about God, the world, and themselves. But their faith also involved "believing in, having confidence in, trusting" God. They placed their faith in God, they relied upon God confidently, giving something more than mere mental assent.

Belief and trust do not exhaust the richness of what is meant by faith—we *know* God forgives us. Calvin defined faith in these words: "We shall possess a right definition of faith if we call it a firm and certain *knowledge* of God's benevolence toward us, founded upon the truth of the freely given promise in Christ, both revealed to our minds and sealed upon our hearts through the Holy Spirit."[10]

Even this assertion does not exhaust the depth of faith. We know that God forgives us in Christ, but we also know God, the One who forgives and addresses us. Such knowledge is unique, powerful, and incredible because it means actually experiencing "God with us," God in our inmost selves. Referring to this phenomenon, a recent report stated:

> The Reformed tradition has spoken of this [knowledge of God] in various ways, but Calvin's formulation, "revealed to our minds and sealed upon our hearts through the Holy Spirit," drives to the heart of being a Christian. Fundamental to our knowing is the stunning fact that we come to know the One who knows us. Christ's "true and efficacious presence" in the Holy Spirit acts in the inner heart and pervades the mind, creating the ultimate condition of our knowing.[11]

Imagine! God knows us, everything about us, and God still loves us; not even our sin can create an impenetrable barrier to that love. This God who comes to us makes that incredible, holy name known to us! We know God, and God's presence actually abides in our consciousness.

In our tradition, God's grace in Christ—Christ alone—has made possible the forgiveness of sin and the creation of a new life. We cannot stress too heavily the uniqueness and absoluteness of Jesus Christ in making God known. According to Calvin, Christ reveals the knowledge of God to us. In him dwelt the fullness of God; he is the image of God, and if we are to be Christian, we must embrace Christ as our only master.[12]

In an age of pluralism, however, many would question the uniqueness of Christ by saying: There are many ways to God, and one way is as good as another. But Jesus said, "No one comes to the Father except through me" (John 14:6). In an age of relativism some hesitate to make Christ absolute. But he said, "I am the way, and the truth, and the life" (John 14:6). And increasingly, the syncretistic spirit of the age has mixed Christ with culture, creating a tame, civil religion. Or Christ has been melded with the Eastern religions to forge a synthetic spirituality. Or Christ has been combined with the organization of the church to form institutional religion. While all these mixtures seem relevant and inclusive, we must not dilute the significance of Christ, the one mediator between God and human beings. In this unique, absolute Christ, Peter and Mary have professed their faith. They are uniting with a congregation that holds this affirmation at the center of its life, as does the church universal. They of course do not know all that this confession will mean for their lives, but it is a "core" confession destined to shape their values and lifestyle.

Our faith in this unique Christ must also be accompanied by repentance. Repentance means "turning," turning from self to God, from sin to righteousness, and from the things of earth to eternal things. Calvin understands repentance to be continuous: "All our life is but one [act] of repentance."

The basic disciplines of the Christian life, according to Calvin, demonstrate this lifestyle of repentance: self-denial, cross bearing, and meditation on the future life. Later we explore these disciplines more thoroughly to see how each occasions our "turning to God" through the material events of our lives.

4. A Christian intends to be Christ's faithful disciple, obeying his word, and showing his love to life's end. When Peter and Mary repeat their vows of membership, God does not

stop working in their lives. God does forgive their sins, but God also continues to nurture their faith and form their lives. God's grace not only forgives, it also empowers us to grow in our faith. This process of growing in the Christian life we call sanctification. Jesus is Savior, but he is also Lord of our life.

Ephesians 4:15–16 teaches that "we must grow up in every way into him who is the head, into Christ, from whom the whole body, joined and knit together by every ligament with which it is equipped, as each part is working properly, promotes the body's growth in building itself up in love." Growth is intrinsic to the Christian life—to be a Christian means to be growing.

The invitation to "grow up into Christ" must not be heard as idle talk but rather as a serious call to become the persons God intended us to be. Forgiveness means continuous growth. As Reformed Christians we do not expect to become perfect, yet by God's grace we must strive for maturity. The old nature remains with us; we never submit completely to the Holy Spirit. Our life is a paradox; the more we grow, the more we become aware that we need to grow.[13]

All Christians belong to the people of God, and God calls each one to a ministry. Officers in the church differ from other members in function only, not in status. The faithful member of the church demonstrates "a new quality of life within and through the church" and lives responsibly in the world.[14]

Practical growth means obedience to Christ. Like Abraham we obey not knowing where our commitment will lead.

Obedience shapes our lives. We love God, we love each other, we love the stranger, we love all creation—such is the nature of our obedience. The love of God and the love of neighbor can be seen clearly in the commandments of God. God gave us two tables of law: the first teaches us to devote ourselves wholly to God, and the second teaches our responsibility toward our fellow human beings. The first table is primary, because our chief end is to glorify God; the second, though secondary in importance, is indispensable because we demonstrate that we really do love God by loving others. To be a Christian, therefore, means to be a faithful disciple by growing in faith, love, and obedience. This kind of growth, in contrast with psychological growth or the search for perfection, leads to maturity in Christ.

5. A Christian belongs to the church, Christ's Body, and promises to participate actively and responsibly in its wor-

ship and mission. Peter and Mary will grow in discipleship and find strength to live out their commitment in the fellowship of God's people. "To be a Christian," says Shirley C. Guthrie, Jr., "is by definition to belong to the church."[15] There is no such thing as a "private Christianity"; Christianity by its very nature demands community.

Christians have long debated whether there can be salvation outside the church. Technically, we know that the church does not save us but rather God's grace in Christ. Thus, although we do not agree that there is no salvation outside the church, we do confess that the church has been indispensable for our salvation.

Too often human pride deceives us with the illusion that we can stand alone and grow alone. American individualism seems bent upon the "loner" approach to religion. A recent survey revealed how deeply embedded in our culture is the idea of churchless Christianity. Of the church dropouts surveyed, 95 percent said they could be "good Christians" without going to church. Nearly two-thirds of those not attending church considered themselves good Christians.[16]

Peter and Mary learned their need for others the hard way. Though they had been baptized as infants and had attended church school for a few years, they drifted away from the church during college. After their marriage they pictured themselves as adequate to meet all life's challenges. They needed no one, so it seemed, as their careers zoomed onward and upward. But then Mary suffered two miscarriages, and Peter's mother died of cancer. The strain of disappointment and grief increased the tension in their marriage. At a crisis point they recognized a need for help. When a man at Peter's office invited him to visit First Church, Peter and Mary decided to give it a try. Both began to realize how far they had strayed from their Christian roots. At First Church they made new friends. With the help of these new friends and the inspiration received in worship, they gained the strength to profess the faith into which they had been baptized. Through the church Peter and Mary experienced genuine faith and began to grow.

Reformed spirituality finds its grounding in the sovereign love of God manifest in creation and in the coming of Jesus Christ. Our reception of that grace begins with faith in God, which is a gift from God. Spirituality develops as faith and love within the fellowship of the church and expresses itself in service to the world. Reformed spirituality is a personal spirituality, a communal spirituality, and a worldly spirituality. Because of the tragic nature of human existence, followers of Christ face throughout life ever new challenges in each of these arenas.

Perhaps it is time to raise the question of personal engagement between the reader and Christ. Where are you in your relation to Christ? A seeker? A believer? A follower? A servant? To grow in your relationship with God, we invite you to take the next step in your life of trust and obedience.

Questions for Reflection

1. What does it mean to be a Christian from a Reformed perspective?
2. How does this perspective compare with that in Baptist churches? Methodist? Roman Catholic? Pentecostal?
3. What is the meaning of spirituality?
4. How does spirituality relate to becoming a Christian?
5. Why do you think many persons are confused about whether or not they are Christians?

See Appendix B for exercises to assist you in appropriating these insights.

2

Spirituality as Response to God's Providence

When Peter and Mary stood before the congregation that warm April Sunday morning, they confessed with the others joining the church, "I believe in God the Father almighty, creator of heaven and earth." Making this statement seemed simple enough at the time, but little did Peter realize the struggle this basic affirmation would bring into his life.

Several months before he and Mary took the vows of church membership, he had made an appointment with Dr. Makemie. In the course of the conversation he explained that his wife had taken courses at a local Christian college and had become passionately interested in religion. He perceived himself to be somewhat irreligious but did not want his lack of faith to discourage her.

"I was reared in the church," he explained, "but when I began attending Tech, most of my childhood faith flew out the window, or more precisely, was extinguished in the classroom."

Dr. Makemie listened sympathetically and asked, "Does this mean that you don't believe in God?"

Shocked by the directness of the question, Peter said, "I don't want to be labeled an unbeliever; it's that I have an analytical, logical mind, and I have never been able to fit faith into a scientific view of the world."

After listening to his struggle with faith, Dr. Makemie gave him *A Brief Statement of Faith,* which the denomination had recently approved, urged him to read it over, and if he could tentatively accept it, to join the church with his wife. She invited Peter to attend the new member class to work out his faith concerns.

In the weeks that followed, Peter struggled with his personal faith in God. Finally he came to a point where he could say with integrity, "I believe in God. . . . " He and Mary decided to profess their faith and to enter into the worship and work of the church.

All went well for several weeks until one Sunday morning when Dr. Makemie preached about the "providential working of God in our everyday lives." For Peter, the closing words of the sermon made a lasting impression:

> As a Christian we must learn
> to accept everything in life
> as from the hand of
> a benevolent heavenly Father!
> Nothing by chance!
> Nothing by accident!
> All within the providence of
> God's gracious love!

Contrast with the Enlightenment Worldview

Peter's struggle, like that of many of us, related to his worldview—how God operates in the world, in the daily experiences of life. Peter is a modern man, a child of the Enlightenment, who in his university training inherited a view of the world which has no place for God. He has united with a Christian church that claims God made the world and providentially guides the course of history and our personal lives. What gave birth to Peter's rationalistic vision of reality? In the sixteenth and seventeenth centuries philosophers dethroned God as the ultimate authority in the universe and substituted human reason in the place of God. Given this commitment to human reason, Enlightenment thought can be summed up in four postulates.

1. God is superfluous. Human beings do not need God to account for anything.
2. Reason is capable of constructing morality.
3. Progress is inevitable.
4. Knowledge is inherently good.

With these postulates philosophers of the Enlightenment created a world that did not depend upon God for its existence, maintenance, or direction. Religion, therefore, became irrelevant if not absurd. By 1878 Max Müller, the distinguished anthropologist, could say, "Every day, every week, every month, every quarter, the most widely read journals seem just now to vie with each other in telling us that the time for religion is past, that faith is a hallucination or an infantile disease, that the gods have at last been exploded."[1]

The Enlightenment mind, for all practical purposes, created a world without God. Persons seduced by this vision lived as if God were not. Still others found themselves living in conflicting worlds—the Sunday world of faith and worship; the Monday world of business, technology, and government. Too many twentieth-century persons still find themselves living with this contradiction.

Presbyterian Christians are not exempt from the conflict— a religious belief in God lived in a world that sees no necessity for God. Is there any hope of deliverance from this double vision and the schizophrenic lifestyle it produces?

At the close of the twentieth century the Enlightenment worldview with its worship of reason has become suspect. Diogenes Allen says, "The foundations of the modern world are collapsing, and we are entering a postmodern world. The principles forged during the Enlightenment (c. 1600–1780), which formed the foundations of the modern mentality, are crumbling."[2]

No longer can respectable intellectuals claim that God is superfluous. Allen suggests there are "developments in philosophy and cosmology that actually point toward God." He further suggests that all efforts to give morality a secular base have become bankrupt with the consequence that "each [person] does what is right in his or her own eyes." With respect to the doctrine of inevitable progress, thinkers have recognized that "evil is real and that it cannot be removed merely by educational and social reform." Allen also says, "Today we are becoming increasingly aware that there is no inherent connection between knowledge and its beneficial use, with genetic engineering just beginning to open new possibilities of abuse, and with the power of bombs and other destructive forces at hand."[3]

If the Enlightenment worldview is collapsing, undermining confidence in the failed god of "reason," what does this mean for the modern Christian? How can Christian men and women influenced by the Enlightenment break out of the emptiness of a mechanistic world and affirm the all-powerful, ever-present God of their faith? This crucial issue faces most modern persons whose worldview has not been inspired by biblical faith—a major issue for a vital spirituality. With confidence we can affirm that John Calvin's understanding of scripture and the faith which it begets certainly calls forth a view of the world in which God is not only alive but active in human affairs.

> Nothing by chance!
> Nothing by accident,
> All within the providence of
> God's gracious love!

These affirmations which jolted Peter at the close of the service of worship have deep roots in the Reformed tradition. The minister's quotation rests upon a belief in the sovereign God who created the world and by divine power providentially guides nations as well as individual lives. An examination of the Reformed belief about creation and providence not only points to the faith underpinning this affirmation but hints at ways persons may become aware of and responsive to this divine presence.

A Biblical Understanding of Creation and Providence

The tradition into which Peter has been baptized claims that God created the cosmos and is revealed in the vastness and the beauty of the creation; it is a mirror through which to contemplate God. The opening words of Genesis testify to God the Creator: "In the beginning when God created the heavens and the earth. . . . " According to the Bible, the creation itself gives testimony to the power and majesty of God:

> The heavens are telling the glory of God;
>   and the firmament proclaims his handiwork.
> Day to day pours forth speech, and night to night
>   declares knowledge.
> There is no speech, nor are there words;
>   their voice is not heard;
> yet their voice goes out through all the earth,
>   and their words to the end of the world.
>   (Psalm 19:1–4)

Ceaselessly, the cosmos pours forth its speech to the ends of the earth, but only those with sensitive ears hear!

In addition to the universe, human beings—special creations of God—testify to God. Scripture states that humans have been made in the image of God: "So God created humankind in his image, in the image of God he created them; male and female he created them" (Gen. 1:27). All the elements of creation are contained in the microcosm of this special creature who exemplifies the goodness, wisdom, and wonder of the Almighty. Calvin said that the human "contains within himself enough miracles to occupy our minds if only we are not irked at paying attention."[4]

This creature in God's image has the capacity to survey heaven and earth, join past to future, sustain in memory something heard long before, and picture to itself whatever it pleases. Calvin suggests that a human "devises things incredible."[5]

But the Reformed tradition does not rest on the mere fact of a Creator. To affirm the Creator of the world alone would leave us with a cold, barren world void of the divine presence—exactly what we have as a consequence of the Enlightenment. The power of God continues to shine through the divine governance of the world as clearly as it does in the creation. Calvin is quite explicit at this point. "For unless we pass on to providence . . . we do not yet properly grasp what it means to say: 'God is Creator.' "[6]

God as creator continues to care for and govern the world. The power of God sustains and nourishes everything that has been created. This mighty Creator is watchful, effective, and engaged in ceaseless activity, not as a general principle preserving the creation but as personal care directed to every individual. In all things this loving God not only sees but acts for our good; God rules the universe with a special care for the order of creation. All things from the rising of the sun, to the melting of snow, to the budding of trees in springtime are moved by "a secret impulse of nature."[7] This watchful care extends especially to humans whose very hairs are numbered.

The Reformed tradition not only affirms that God sustains and nourishes human beings and all of creation but that God has a controlling purpose operative in nature and in human affairs. This mighty God makes the winds into messengers and flaming fire his ministers; the clouds are the Lord's chariots, and the Lord rides on the wind; God makes barren and gives the power to procreate.[8] These convictions may be too strong for some of Calvin's followers. Yet he certainly believed that "nothing happens except by his command or permission."[9] We are not, however, privy to all the ways of the Lord— so many things remain "hidden" in the secret wisdom of God.

Calvin claimed that even evildoers are agents of God's providence. But let us be clear, God does not will evil. As Shirley C. Guthrie, Jr., says, "We shall see that God is powerful enough to use evil and turn it to his own purposes. He can make good come out of evil. But we cannot say that God is the author of evil. Evil is by definition what God does not will and does not do. There is no secret identity between God and the Devil!"[10]

The strong belief in providence stems from the power and majesty of Almighty God, the Creator and Sustainer of all. This mighty Creator constantly pours out the fullness of divine presence into the natural world and governs the affairs of societies and communities so that the divine will is done. While this tradition sustains persons in persecution and hardship and buttresses the anxious soul against the abyss of meaninglessness, it perhaps overlooks one aspect of the revelation of God, the biblical witness to God's vulnerability.

The Bible further testifies to a God revealed in weakness.[11] When God chose to reveal godself to us, the Son emptied himself of divine prerogatives and was made in the likeness of a human; and in the form of a man, he humbled himself and became obedient even unto death (see Phil. 2:5–11). In the incarnation and in the crucifixion we encounter a God who has willingly become weak, humble, and vulnerable.

The Reformed tradition based on the power and majesty of God must be blended with the biblical revelation of a crucified God who became vulnerable to humans, identified with them, and redeemed all creation through suffering. We can never understand the fullness of the revelation of God until we see God's absolute power in the light of God's willingness to become weak for our sake!

We must also consider human freedom. Is our choice of no consequence? Has the Creator not shared with us the power to decide and act freely? If freedom is an illusion, how can we be held accountable? When questioned, a staunch Calvinist friend of ours said, "Two things are true: humans are free and God is sovereign. Both are true, and this is paradoxical!"

This explanation of the faith which supports Dr.

Makemie's affirmation—"nothing by chance; nothing by accident"—may not answer all the questions relating to freedom and providence. It does make clear one thing—God is present and active in the world, in everything that touches our lives. The world revealed in the Word of God stands in bold contrast to the cold, empty, lonely world of the Enlightenment. Reformed spirituality calls us to an awareness of the presence of God in the world and in our personal lives and to a response of love, gratitude, and obedience.

Calvin's Testimony

We have often wondered how John Calvin would have given personal testimony to his faith in providence, which he so carefully wove into the tradition. Since only scant personal testimony exists, we think the following witness could very well describe his experience of grace and his trust in the providential goodness of God.

Whether this imaginative reconstruction accurately relates Calvin's testimony or not, it intends to capture the elements that shaped his conviction about the nature of the world and God's activity in it. Perhaps this statement of faith can help us live with greater sensitivity to the divine presence in our history.

I, John Calvin

My father intended me to study theology but realized that I would always be poor, so he directed me to study law. Being obedient to my father's wishes I began the study of law, but God in his secret providence turned my course another way. At the time of this shift, I was immersed in the religious superstitions of my upbringing from which I was rescued by God's sovereign grace.

Since childhood I had a profound religious hunger, though clouded with superstition. The church had rightly taught me the existence of God, though I did not know God's character or nature. But when I surveyed the vastness of the heavens, the orderliness of the stars, and the magnificence of the creation, I was gripped with an unshakable conviction of the presence and power of Almighty God.

This conviction of God deepened when I contemplated the wonders of the creation and of my own nature, so complex and so intricately woven together. How amazed was I to discover that something within me could scan the past and discover the mighty work of God in the occurrences of life and then weave the meaning into a common piece with the happenings of the present moment. While my mental powers could never grasp this infinite God, I was often gripped in amazement by the Divine Majesty. To look upon myself drove me immediately to think of God, of my weakness and vulnerability first and then of God's immeasurable greatness.

Through God's sovereign mercy I experienced a sudden conversion. God brought my heart into submission. Such joy and gratitude filled me that I have never been able to describe it fully. Furthermore, I have been shy about exposing my deepest feelings.

As I have reviewed my personal history, the vastness of the universe and the complexity of the human creature, these reflections have buttressed my confidence in the Creator. As I read the scriptures, I realized that the same power which sustained and directed the universe guided my life. Because of God's sovereign power I came to believe that nothing is by chance, that everything is a bearer of God's will.

With the confidence that life is lived out of his fatherly hand, I began a careful reflection upon the course of my life as did my mentor Augustine before me. Unlike him, I did not have the courage to expose directly the depths of my sinful self, so I disguised this personal truth in my descriptions of fallen human nature and my warnings against the flesh.

In the course of my reflections I became more and more convinced of the direction of God's fatherly hand in my life. Convinced of God's divine majesty, power, and pervasive presence, I learned to trust that everything in my life came not only through the divine permission but by the divine command. This absolute confidence in the providence of God never once caused me to cease from study, thought, and action. Rather, I have been immeasurably strengthened by the assurance that I am so engaged by the will of God to the glory of God![12]

Responding to God's Providence

How can Peter and Mary live in an awareness of God, in response to God's goodness and graciousness? How can they live in this new world of the Spirit with its dynamics, its power, and its values, rather than in the one-dimensional materialistic world to which they have become accustomed? The decision to join the church brought them face to face with a new world about which they knew very little. How were they to engage this world? How would they live in response to its power? Their predicament parallels that of many church members—they believe, they belong, but they do not know how to recognize and respond to the God who intervenes in history.

Yet, one thread runs through the whole of Reformed spirituality—fellowship with God in all of life; it occurs through an awareness of and a responsiveness to the reality of the Creator who providentially orders our common life. If God is present here and now, if divine power constantly sustains our lives, and if nothing has been left to chance, how are we to live in response to this God who acts in our lives?

We have already hinted that the tradition offers clues about receiving and responding to God's presence. Calvin claimed that humans have enough miracles within themselves to inspire confidence in God "if they are not irked at paying attention." We must pay attention to our lives, Calvin suggested, and use our capacity to survey heaven and earth, join past to future, retain experiences, picture the future, and devise incredible things. What is this but awareness, reason, memory, imagination, and ingenuity? A discussion of several of these faculties will provide helpful clues about how we can pay attention to God's will and presence in our lives.

One doorway to growth can be entered by *awareness*. And what is awareness but that uniquely human capacity which, though broken, bears the mark of the divine? We have the ability to notice, to be aware of our being. If God has created us and in every moment of existence sustains us, the very thought of our being inspires wonder. What a wonder I am, that I exist by the power of an almighty creator God!

Perhaps one of the most devastating consequences of the Enlightenment has been the smothering of wonder and with it the capacity for awe and reverence. Is there anything closer to religious impulse than the capacity to wonder?

Our awareness of past and future provides the matrix for the creation of meaning. Meaning refers to the constructive joining of past to future in the present so that life has movement, continuity, and direction. Without a sense of meaning human beings cannot exist. Spirituality feeds off the awareness of what occurs in our world and in the events of our personal lives. Our faith in God enables us to make sense of what happens and maintain a sense of purpose in the face of calamities.

Such meaning depends upon *memory* of the past and provides yet another clue for discerning God's will and presence in our lives. With the marvelous capacities of reflection and meditation God has given us, we are able to pull out of memory the major events in our lives. Viewing these events through the lens of faith yields remarkable new insights. Through contemplation, we realize that God has indeed been shaping the events of our lives without our knowing it.

Not in memory only do we perceive the benevolence of God's "fatherly hand," but also in very ordinary occurrences, like the visit of a friend, the chance meeting with an old acquaintance, a job offer, or an invitation to a party. Thus, in some unplanned event, we are made aware of divine goodness, of mercy shown, of a purpose at work beyond our own.

If this "fatherly God" works in our memories of the past and the events of the present, certainly this loving God is active in our imaginations regarding the future. We humans can "devise incredible things." Thus *imagination* is a final clue showing us the way to God's will and presence. As we imagine, we envision an alternative world to one of greed and violence; we envision a way of life free from addiction and materialism; and we picture life lived in harmony with the intention of the Creator.

And where do hopes and dreams come from? Must we consign all these to a "fallen, corrupted, sinful" soul? Without discounting the pervasiveness of our sinfulness, surely God's Spirit stirs the depths of the human spirit to dream dreams of the divine will! Must we not pay attention to our hopes and dreams as faulty, but at times effective, mediators of the divine will in our lives?

These marvelous capacities of the soul—awareness, memory, and imagination—provide data enough to awaken us to the adventure provoked by divine providence. Through these clues we become aware of God at work in our lives, retain in memory many personal incidents in which God was present, and by our imaginations devise incredible things which point to God's will. If we begin the journey with an awareness created by the Spirit, we can count on this gracious, sovereign God to guide us toward our destiny.

Those of us in transition from a cold, mechanical world to a warm, God-directed one have little difficulty believing in the presence of the living God until . . . until some evil or tragic event contradicts our expectation of a gracious loving God. A godly man is struck down by cancer, a child is born deformed, thousands of persons are crushed by an earthquake, and then we ask, "Where now is the God who is full of grace and love?"

Calvin had no acknowledged difficulty with these occur-rences. He explained that nothing occurred through chance, that everything has been willed by God for our good. If we cannot see the good, our blindness only indicates that we do not know God's secret purposes.

Some who follow in this tradition have difficulty assigning "everything" to God's design and active will. These Calvinists would also strongly resist the notion that history has been left to chance. Somewhere between these two ex-tremes lies the truth of God's providence. Truly, nothing can occur without God, for apart from God nothing even exists. But to say that God permits evil or uses evil for good seems to us a very different statement from saying, "God wills it." We are willing to say: Nothing comes to us without God's pres-ence—God is in everything. Nothing comes to us without God's permission—God is sovereign. Nothing comes to us which cannot be made to serve God's sovereign purpose— "We know that all things work together for good for those who love God . . . " (Rom. 8:28).[13]

Reformed spirituality, therefore, builds on the twin foun-dations of grace and providence. We become Christians through God's unmerited love—God elects us and redeems us. This kindness we receive through faith.

But God does not re-create us to abandon us to our own wits; rather, God comes to us in all the events of our lives. If nothing occurs through chance, if there are no accidents, then everything that happens to us provides substance for our spirituality, and our faithful response to life shapes our spiri-tuality. In contrast to denying the world or escaping from the world, Reformed spirituality embraces the world with all its occurrences as a bearer of God's presence and will. Life itself, therefore, provides a medium of fellowship with God and participation with God in expressing the Kingdom.

The two foundations for the development of a Reformed spirituality have been labeled: the profession of Christian faith and a confidence in the living God active in our history. This life of faith requires nourishment, and the means of grace for continuous growth are found in worship, prayer, scripture, and the sacraments. We will examine these in the following section.

Questions for Reflection

1. What are the characteristics of the modern world? Upon what are they based?
2. How does this worldview affect the development of one's spirituality?
3. How does a biblical view of the world compare and contrast with the Enlightenment worldview?
4. Is God in everything? Give reasons for your answer.
5. How can persons become more aware of God in their lives?

MEANS OF GRACE FOR THE CHRISTIAN LIFE

3

Worship
as Spiritual
Formation

Meredith Ann Wilson, who joined First Church with Peter and Mary, had attended for six months before deciding to join. Her entry into the church came through an invitation to be the soprano soloist in the choir. She accepted because she wished to use her talent for the glory of God.

For more than five years Meredith Ann had been divorced. Rearing a seven-year-old daughter required hard work and careful management of money. Much of Meredith Ann's life seemed routine, but singing in the choir boosted her spirit; she had also begun to find acceptance and support from the other choir members.

Before joining First Church, however, Meredith Ann had to resolve her difficulty with the form and style of worship. For most of her twenty-nine years she had worshiped in a black church that seemed to praise God with more freedom, self-expression, and spontaneity. Increasingly, she felt a dryness in worship at First Church that failed to nurture her spirit.

One day she heard herself wondering aloud, "'Is it I, or is the worship dead?'"

She took her growing concern to Dr. Makemie. "Dr. M.," she began, "I've been troubled recently about my experience, really the lack of it, in worship. Is something wrong with me, or is the service lacking in spirit?"

"Well, I suppose it could be a bit of both," Dr. Makemie responded. "It could also be a lack of understanding of worship and of our particular style in the Presbyterian Church."

Aware that a number of new members in the past few years had joined First Church from other Christian traditions, and further aware that each had unconsciously assumed that "my way is the right way," Sarah Makemie decided to offer an evening seminar on Reformed worship. She realized that worship offered a means of grace to persons, and if they did not understand the form, they could not participate wholeheartedly and live their faith enthusiastically in the world of ordinary experience.

Like Meredith Ann Wilson, many of us go through the motions of worship without experiencing its true meaning. In an effort to assist those nurtured in another tradition or no tradition, or those who have taken for granted the Reformed tradition, we will explore the importance of worship, the distinctive features of Reformed worship, and how each of us can make worship a means of grace in our lives.

The Importance of Worship

Worship of God has always been at the heart of the Reformed tradition. Calvin underscored its importance when he counseled us "to contemplate, fear, and worship [God's] majesty; to participate in his blessings; to seek his help at all times; to recognize, and by praises to celebrate, the greatness of his works—as the only goal of all the activities of this life."[1]

To say that worship is the *only* goal of all the activities of this life, as Calvin said, puts worship in a new perspective. It hardly makes public worship optional for the Christian. Nor does it make daily personal worship a "take it or leave it" proposition. Quite the contrary! Worshiping God becomes crucial for living the Christian life. As we praise God and recite the drama of grace, we are renewed. We receive the strength we need to go and make disciples, to serve the needy, to work for justice and peace, and to care for all creation. How can we continue to minister without praising God from whom all blessings flow?

Worship, therefore, ranks first as a means of grace. A contemporary report on a Reformed understanding of the Christian faith says that worship is first "because it is the central and orienting practice of the Christian life."[2] Worship of God provides the context and purpose for all that Christians are and do.

Meredith Ann Wilson would have no trouble agreeing that worship is the central and orienting practice of the Christian life. However, she still might not understand the distinctive qualities in Reformed worship.

Distinctive Aspects of Reformed Worship

Reformed worship is marked by a central focus on God, is informed and guided by scripture, recognizes preaching and prayer as being at the heart of worship, is personal and communal, and intends to build up people in the faith. These distinctive qualities might affirm and expand Meredith Ann Wilson's style of worship.

Reformed worship is marked by a central focus on the triune God. True worship acknowledges the Trinitarian nature of God whom alone we worship as God. An exclusive focus on God abolishes every form of idolatry. Although we bring our lives—our total life experience—into worship, we do not concentrate on our experience. We envision God, "high and lofty," and seek to worship the One in whom "we live and move and have our being" (Acts 17:28). Elevating God does not exclude an experience of the divine in worship, but rather shifts the focus from the worshipers to God. Would this principle be of help to Meredith Ann as well as to us?

Scripture informs and guides our worship. Scripture provides the basis for our faith and practice, the touchstone of all that we do. As such, the Bible calls us to worship a sovereign, loving God who is "high and lofty" (Isa. 6:1), "though indeed he is not far from each one of us" (Acts 17:27). As God met Isaiah in the temple "in the year that King Uzziah died" (Isa. 6:1), we believe God meets us in worship. Similarly, God illumines us when we worship, convicts us of our sin, forgives us, calls us to action, and invites us to respond. As God met Moses at the burning bush, so God meets us in our worship, filling us with awe and wonder, summoning us to confront the Pharaohs of our day. As God met a Samaritan woman at the well through her encounter with Jesus, God also meets us, teaching us also to "worship the Father in spirit and truth" (John 4:23). Although Reformed worship affords freedom and flexibility, most liturgists prefer scripture in every element, from the call to worship to the benediction. The use of scripture, the hallmark of the Reformed style, focuses on the texts of scripture as the form and content of divine worship. This intentional focus helps avoid humanly constructed, manipulative forms of worship.

Preaching is an important means of grace. The Reformation once again unleashed the enormous power of preaching, and Calvin had no peer as an interpreter and proclaimer of scripture. John H. Leith contends that preaching, for Calvin, "was the means of grace above all others by which he expected God to transform Geneva."[3] The preaching in corporate worship aims to inform our personal worship as well as our daily life. The preached word intends to transform the mind and inspire the heart so that worshipers may live a life rooted and grounded in Jesus Christ.

Reformed worship is communal and personal in nature. The Reformed church, more than most, has insisted that personal worship, in all of its forms, is inseparably linked to the life and public worship of the church. The very practices of our daily personal devotions are couched in the language and forms of the corporate worship of the church. For example, as we pray for our needs, we are inevitably led to pray for the whole family of heaven and earth.[4] Personal prayer takes its form from communal worship. A dynamic synergy exists between these two forms; personal worship enhances communal worship and communal worship shapes and forms personal worship. Prominent linkage between these two aspects exists in the Lord's Prayer.

Worship in the Reformed tradition offers edification. Liturgy is for life. According to John Leith, Calvin claimed that "the form of liturgy that he presented to the church was 'entirely directed toward edification.' "[5] Thus, the acid test of Reformed worship is whether it increases love of God and neighbor. Worship should lead to holiness of life. We worship God, however, not because we are holy but because *God* is holy. A vision of God's holiness strengthens us and leads us to bear fruit in the world by doing God's will.[6]

Reformed worship gives a significant place to the sacraments of baptism and the Lord's Supper. Through worship the sacraments seal the word of God upon our hearts. This sealing refers to a "guarantee," like the seal of a notary public. In our personal worship we prepare to receive the sacraments by prayer and self-examination. Every baptism, for example, affords us an opportunity to renew our profession of faith in Jesus Christ. Each Lord's Supper invites us to sit at table with Jesus and to be nourished by his broken body and shed blood.

How does the character of Reformed worship affect the way Meredith Ann or any of us worships God? We enter the house of God with our central focus on God, not on our expected experience but on God's glory. In the words of scripture we find a means of expressing our worship. We cultivate the idea that our worship has two aspects—public and private. Even when we worship in private, we do so as a member of the congregation. We receive the body and blood of Christ in faith, believing that he does forgive and accept us and that his presence is as real as bread in our hands or wine on our lips. This character of Reformed worship challenges us more deeply to make the worship of God central to our lives.

Our Worship

Suppose you had an invitation from the president of the United States to attend a formal dinner at the White House. How would this opportunity affect you? Would not anyone with an invitation to dine with the president prepare for the visit by having the proper attire, the appropriate protocol, and the right frame of mind?

If you were served a dinner of veal cordon bleu, could you imagine sitting there and not eating? Certainly you would join the group, enjoy the food, and share in the fellowship.

And suppose the dinner concluded with a pledge of allegiance to the flag. This patriotic ritual would join you with other citizens and reinforce your loyalty to your country.

Consider how the invitation to worship God calls us to prepare, to participate, and to let the spirit of worship pervade our lives. Like a citizen invited to a White House dinner, we must prepare ourselves for worship lest we be like the guest who went to the banquet without proper attire. (See Matt. 22:11–14.) To prepare for worship we need to review all the blessings we have received from God's hand. Thinking about God's blessings puts us in the proper frame of mind for worship. All of us have needs and problems, which we take to God in worship. Although we may be motivated to go to church out of a sense of need, we do not worship primarily to deal with our needs and problems. We worship to praise and honor the Holy One of Israel, who is the source of all blessings, including life itself. But as we focus our attention on God, we cannot help also addressing our own needs.

We also prepare for worship by examining ourselves. Often we discover the sin that separates us from God and the specific practices that keep us from fellowship with God. By asking for mercy before we worship and during the service itself, we clear our ears to hear the word of God.

Preparation for worship also includes study and meditation on the scriptures, especially those to be used in the Sunday service. Some churches announce to the congregation in advance the passages of scripture to be read and proclaimed. Reflection on the text develops in worshipers a sense of expectancy and interest they would not otherwise have. Even if the church does not announce the scripture texts in advance, the daily study of scripture will prepare our hearts for worship. Biblical truth informs the service; it also helps us worship.

Prayer also prepares us for worship. Pray for those in the congregation who particularly need God's help. Pray for the ministers and their families. Pray for yourself that you may worship God in spirit and in truth. Pray for the world and the ministry of the church in, to, and with the world.

Do not self-examination, reflection on the text, and prayer create an atmosphere of worship in our hearts? The spirit of worship prepares us to meet God and to bring praise and glory to God's name.

Like a guest at a White House dinner who joyously partakes of the food, we participate in the worship of God. Too many worshipers fail to find worship meaningful because they, for whatever reason, do not participate. When the congregation sings, they make half-hearted attempts. During the prayer of confession they carefully conceal the sins that keep them awake at night. They feel more comfortable when led to confess in general, "We all like sheep have gone astray." When the minister preaches, they listen just long enough to see whether they will be entertained. And when the ushers pass the offering plate, they fail to offer either themselves or their money. Little wonder the service of worship does not excite them!

A Reformed Order of Worship

Worshipers need not be half-hearted in their worship. By understanding and participating in the order of service we can worship with more meaning and power. Consider the order of worship for the Lord's Day.[7] Understanding the components of worship enables full participation.

Gathering Around the Word

When we gather for worship, our worship begins. We are called to worship through words of scripture which announce God's gracious acts. Then we respond by praising God for such gracious acts. As we hear God's promises of love and forgiveness, we dare to confess our sins and receive God's pardon. We turn to our fellow Christians, sharing signs of our reconciliation and the peace of Christ. Forgiven and reconciled to one another, we are now prepared to hear the proclamation of the Word of God.

Proclaiming the Word

The minister leads us in a prayer seeking the illumination of God's Spirit as scripture is read, proclaimed, and heard. Appropriate lessons from scripture include readings from the Old Testament, epistles, and gospels. Usually the minister proclaims the word in a sermon, calling us to renewed discipleship. We participate in the sermon by active, expectant listening.

Responding to the Word

Having heard the minister proclaim the word, we now respond. We often say or sing a creed of the church, making use of rich creedal and confessional resources like the Apostles' Creed. We may also respond by renewing our baptismal vows or by being commissioned for service in the church, such as teaching in the church school. Sometimes we commemorate significant transitions in our lives or hear the mission of the church presented. The minister or liturgist voices the intercessory prayers on our behalf for the hurts, hungers, and hopes of the world, as well as prayers of supplication for the needs of our church. Then we gratefully respond to God's grace by giving our tithes and offerings. As we do so, we rededicate our lives to God.

The Sealing of the Word: Sacraments

Now we are ready for God's sealing acts in baptism and the Lord's Supper. Children and adults may receive baptism, which seals the promise of God's grace proclaimed in the sermon. Though we may have been baptized long ago, we can renew our own baptismal vows. All who have been baptized and trust in Christ may be sealed in God's covenant of grace by participating in the Lord's Supper. As we partake, we experience the presence of the risen Christ, nourishing our faith and joining us in the communion of the saints.

Bearing and Following the Word Into the World

We who have gathered in God's name are now dismissed to go in God's name to love and serve the risen Christ. Before the minister gives the charge and benediction, we may choose to make acts of commitment or be recognized for accepting new church roles and responsibilities. The gracious God who called us together now sends us forth in the power of the Spirit.

When Meredith Ann Wilson and all of us leave church to return to our daily routines, we bear and follow the word of God into the world. Liturgy and life go together. Without liturgy, our lives will be powerless; without life our liturgy will be irrelevant.

Too often we leave our commitment at the church door. As the days roll by, we may forget our intentions so freely offered during corporate worship. We may need to conduct a midweek obedience check. Read the scripture again. Review the sermon. Remember your intentions. And when you fall short, ask for forgiveness.

Worship is a means of grace that nurtures our faith so that we may be servants of the Lord in the common tasks of life. Jesus Christ, the living Word, meets us not only when we sing the doxology but also when we sit in a tense board room or ride a commuter train. The service of worship and our service in the world deepen our awareness of God and our participation in the reign of God. As a Reformed Christian, then, we will concern ourselves with reverence for God and love for neighbor.

In the next chapter we examine another means of grace for living the Christian life—prayer.

Questions for Reflection

1. Why does worship stand at the center of Reformed spirituality?
2. What different elements enter into the worship of God? What does each element signify?
3. In what way does worship form one's spirituality? Nurture one's spirituality?
4. How does worship relate to our common life in the world?
5. How could worship in your church be enlivened?

4

Prayer
as a Means
of Grace

During the new members class when Peter and Mary were preparing for church membership, an incident occurred that surprised the whole class. In the midst of a discussion on worship, Albert Mustain asked, "Dr. Makemie, do you really believe it makes any difference whether or not we pray?"

The question came with such suddenness that Sarah Makemie consciously struggled to keep her composure. She answered Al's question briefly and at that moment decided to schedule a day-long seminar on prayer and spiritual growth.

Several months later at the first session of the seminar Dr. Makemie greeted each member by name and opened the seminar with prayer. She began by saying, "I believe in prayer; it is the lifeblood of the Reformed tradition and the whole of Christian faith. It is one of the chief ways God helps us grow in the life of faith."

She then quoted Karl Barth, who said, "Prayer is a grace, an offer of God."[1] For us to benefit from prayer, we must accept and act upon God's gracious offer. Dr. Makemie said that it was important to explore the Reformed teaching on prayer, the attitude we bring to prayer, and some decisions we need to make about prayer. Much of what we believe, of course, we share with all Christians.

To help the class begin thinking about prayer, Dr. Makemie wrote a contemporary statement about prayer on the chalk board and asked for each class member's reaction.

> Prayer is at the heart of worship. In prayer, through the Holy Spirit, people seek after and are found by the one true God who has been revealed in Jesus Christ. They listen and wait for

47

God, call God by name, remember God's gracious acts, and offer themselves to God. Prayer may be spoken, sung, offered in silence, or enacted. Prayer grows out of the center of a person's life in response to the Spirit. Prayer is shaped by the Word of God in Scripture and by the life of the community of faith. Prayer issues in commitment to join God's work in the world.[2]

Dr. Makemie gave the class a few minutes to formulate their responses. When she opened the floor for discussion, she received the following questions:

"Does God really hear all our prayers, even those unspoken desires present in our hearts?"

"Does prayer affect the outcome of things? Will not God do right whether we pray or not?"

"If prayer includes dialogue, how do we learn to listen?"

"How can we receive help in forming prayers in an acceptable manner?"

"Are there biblical guidelines for our prayers?"

"What about a model? Is there a pattern for us to follow?"

As Dr. Makemie listened to these fundamental questions regarding prayer, she realized the seriousness with which each had been asked. She began to think about how to answer from the perspective of the Reformed tradition. She told the class they would examine the foundation of prayer and explore practical ways to begin a life of prayer.

The Foundation of Prayer

If we are to grasp the meaning of Reformed spirituality, we must always examine the theological perspective that informs it. In this context the term "theological perspective" means how our view of God relates to prayer. The test of prayer in the Reformed tradition will not be how well it works, or how it makes us feel, but whether it is according to the will of God. Therefore we examine our foundational beliefs about God and how they inform prayer. What are those beliefs?

First, God hears and answers prayer. If God hears prayer, we ought to pray; if God answers prayer, we ought to listen! Barth recognized that the Reformers, particularly Calvin, made the basic point that God does answer prayer. "God," says Barth, "is not deaf, he listens; more than that, he acts."[3] What could be more basic to prayer than the conviction that we are heard by God?

But can prayer really change God? We cannot manipulate God or control God, but influencing God is another matter. God incorporates our requests into the divine will. Barth says, "God is certainly immutable. But He is immutable as the living God and in the mercy in which He espouses the cause of the creature. In distinction from the immovability of a supreme idol, His majesty . . . consists in the fact that He can give to the requests of His creature a place in His will."[4] In the economy of God a place for human desire and prayer has been firmly set. Unless human beings pray, some things will not be accomplished!

Immutable does not mean unresponsive. In God's divine sovereignty our prayers have a place in the governance of the world. God makes room for our requests in the divine will. Barth even says elsewhere that God "does not act in the same way whether we pray or not. Prayer exerts an influence upon God's action, even upon his existence. This is what the word 'answer' means."[5] Human prayer means something to God. Does this not inspire us to pray? If God takes seriously the longings of creatures as well as their praises, can there be any greater incentive to pray? Are we not moved by the thought that our feeble prayers have an influence upon God and affect the governance of the universe?

But there is another aspect of prayer. If prayer is genuine dialogue—and the Reformed tradition says it is—we must listen as well as speak. Persons who never listen are poor conversationalists. Too often we think of our relationship with God as a one-way street: we talk, and God listens and answers. Many definitions of prayer convey this idea. The Larger Catechism says, "Prayer is an offering up of our desires unto God . . . "[6] This way of defining prayer says nothing about listening to God or waiting upon God. For too long we have stressed talking to God to the neglect of listening to God.

Not only do we believe God hears prayer, we also believe Jesus Christ mediates our prayers. Prayer must be in the name of Jesus Christ, our Mediator. Calvin contended that we are unworthy to come to God in our own name and says that God "has given us his Son, Jesus Christ our Lord, to be our Advocate [1 John 2:1] and Mediator with him [1 Tim. 2:5; cf. Heb. 8:6 and 9:15], by whose guidance we may confidently come to him, and with such an intercessor, trusting nothing we ask in his name will be denied us, as nothing can be denied to him by the Father."[7]

For Barth, "Our prayers have already been prayed on our behalf by our Mediator. We enjoy access to God through him, and through him we are able to enter God's presence, where, 'fundamentally, our prayer is already made even before we formulate it.' "[8]

What an amazing vision of Christ! To think that Christ attends our hearts so closely that he knows our desires before we have verbalized them. When we give voice to them, they arise to God in concert with those spoken by Christ on our behalf. And so we pray confidently, knowing we are joined by Christ Jesus.

By faith we have received Christ into our lives; he abides in the depths of our consciousness and inspires in us the prayer that he prays in the presence of God. We are comforted by having such an understanding and all-sufficient Mediator.

Our emphasis on Christ the Mediator, especially as one who works in our hearts, leads to yet another affirmation: The Holy Spirit instructs us in our prayers. We cannot pray properly by relying on the spontaneous impulses of our own feelings.[9] Paul's word to the Romans makes this point: "Likewise the Spirit helps us in our weakness; for we do not know how to pray as we ought, but that very Spirit intercedes with sighs too deep for words" (Rom. 8:26).

How desperately we need the help of the Spirit! Sometimes we cannot focus our minds and hearts intently upon God. In those times God gives us the Spirit to help us. It is not that the Spirit "actually prays or groans but arouses in us assurance, desires, and sighs, to conceive which our natural powers would scarcely suffice."[10]

If the Spirit so directs our petitions and intercessions, can we not rely also on the Spirit to speak in our silence? When we listen the Spirit may flash new insight and guide our imagination as a form of God's speech to us. The ministry of the Spirit is indispensable in our prayers.

But how are we to pray to this God who answers prayer? The scriptures provide the substance of our prayer; they inspire our prayer; and they offer us the perfect form of prayer. God provides scripture to ground and shape our prayer. "In order to be a genuine exercise of faith," writes Ronald S. Wallace, "prayer must be founded upon the Word of God. The faith that gives rise to prayer is created by the Word and is ever aroused to fresh life and vigour by listening to the promises of the Word."[11] Scripture should do more than precede and inspire our approach to prayer; it should also govern the direction and details of our prayer. When we pray according to God's Word, our prayers echo God's promises in our hearts.

Not only is scripture the substance of our prayers, it inspires our prayers. Calvin believed hearing the Word of God led naturally to prayer. How can anyone be confronted with the claims of God and the promises of God without having a prayerful heart?

The scriptures also give us a model for our prayers. This model, the Lord's Prayer, is perfect and complete and should be properly used. The Lord's Prayer is the perfect prayer. Calvin praised it extravagantly, saying, "This prayer is in all respects so perfect that any extraneous or alien thing added to it, which cannot be related to it, is impious and unworthy to be approved by God."[12]

The model prayer directs three petitions to God—God's name, God's kingdom, and God's will. Three petitions refer to us: daily bread, forgiveness for our sins, deliverance from evil. The model first concerns God, but it does not leave out our needs.[13]

Yet the Lord's Prayer, as complete as it is, should not restrict us. Many prayers in scripture differ greatly from the Lord's Prayer, yet they were written by the same Spirit of God. The Spirit inspires different prayers in believers today. We judge our prayers by the Lord's Prayer, but do not limit ourselves to it.

Does this view of prayer shed light on the questions raised by Dr. Makemie's class? The nature of God as one who both wills and hears prayer provides the foundation of prayer. The scriptures, the Spirit, and especially the model prayer help us create the form and content of our prayers.

The Manner of Prayer

If God hears and answers prayer, how do we come to God? Surely our prayer will be ineffective unless we come in faith, believing that our prayers will succeed. Prayer should follow in the footsteps of faith, believing the teaching of Christ who said, "So I tell you, whatever you ask for in prayer, believe that you have received it, and it will be yours" (Mark 11:24).

Prayers arising from the desires of our hearts must be qualified as Jesus suggested: "If in my name you ask me for anything, I will do it" (John 14:14). Selfish requests cannot be

made "in the name" of Jesus. "To pray in the name of Christ
is . . . to ask mercy for his sake: not by the bare mentioning of
his name; but by drawing our encouragement to pray, and our
boldness, strength, and hope of acceptance in prayer, from
Christ and his mediation."[14] God will not honor selfish requests, prayers of revenge, or anything contrary to the nature
of Christ. Prayer in his name means in the spirit, the will, and
the person of Jesus. That form of believing prayer God will
honor.

Reformed prayer has always been characterized by boldness. The Word of God with its sure promises of God's grace
begets boldness of spirit, and boldness demonstrates faith, a
faith that receives an answer from God.

In view of all we know about God and the role of Christ and
the gift of the Holy Spirit, how can we not believe? God desires
our prayer and will answer our prayer. Fervent prayer is the only
proper response to God's promise to hear and answer.

We contend that prayer must include petition—asking God
for what we need. Not only is petition commanded, but it also
shows our dependence upon God. We emphatically reject the
notion that petition has no true place in prayer.

Are not there reasons enough to convince us to bring our
needs to God? How often have we neglected to ask for forgiveness, reconciliation with a brother or sister, strength for a
task, help with a temptation, or guidance for the future? Let
us boldly present these needs before God with the sure confidence that God cares about us and our needs. As you pray,
recall that these requests have already been in the prayer of
our Lord in your behalf.

Jesus seems to go even further in describing the content of
our prayer. It is "whatever you ask for in prayer," Jesus says
(Mark 11:24). He includes not only our needs but also our
desires. Can the Holy Spirit also inspire within our hearts
those desires which harmonize with God's will, desires about
which Christ already knows? How can it be otherwise if our
deepest desires have already been spoken by Christ?

Laying bare our heart before God requires a strong confidence in God's grace. This faith dissolves pretense, draws us
out of hiding, and heals our most shameful parts. We have a
tendency to suppress our fears and griefs, to keep our sorrow to
ourselves, and to complain to our fellow human beings rather
than to God. Let us learn to cast our burdens on God in prayer.

Our prayer includes thanksgiving. "In giving thanks, cele-brate with due praise his benefits toward us, and credit to his generosity every good that comes to us."[15] As Calvin suggests, we have no right to use the benefits of God without recogniz-ing from whence they come. Gratitude tops the list of Chris-tian virtues.

Someone asked Barth how he knew he was a Christian. He reportedly said, "Because I am grateful."[16] If at times our prayer seems cold and forced, let us begin to name all the blessings of our lives. Note how quickly our hearts are warmed and how freely our prayers flow. Perhaps the Holy Spirit uses gratitude to fuel the movement of prayer.

We come to God in faith; we come in need; we come in gratitude; and we come in intercession for others, showing our love for them through our prayers. God does not intend for us to become so bogged down in our personal problems that we do not care about others; rather, our personal sorrows are intended by God to lead us into a greater concern for the whole church and the reign of God.

Is there any work greater than intercession? God has made a place for our prayers; God desires our prayers; perhaps a part of God's intention for the church and the manifestations of the reign of God await the prayers of God's people. How crucial it is for us, therefore, to search for new ways, public and private, to make intercession for the church and the world.

Finally, our prayer must include discipline and persever-ance. A life of prayer is enormously difficult, as anyone who has tried it can attest. The problems are legion: how to estab-lish a routine and overcome wandering thoughts, doubts about the value of prayer, neglect, personal resistance, and spiritual dryness. Maybe prayer should be as natural as breathing, but it is not. The mature life of prayer depends upon a special grace to persevere through all the temptations and pitfalls that distract us.

Though discipline and perseverance may sound like words for a bygone era, they are often what we need most. We believe in an orderly life as a corrective to the permissive, "follow your feelings" climate of today. Left to our own inclinations, our prayer would likely become nonexistent. Our discipline should include both public and private prayer. In private prayer we open ourselves to God whether or not we feel like praying, whether or not the Holy Spirit instructs us to pray, and whether or not the scriptures inspire us. Persistence takes discipline!

A Model of Reformed Prayer

Our exploration of the foundation and the manner of prayer leaves yet the question of method. How do we begin to pray? Prayer commends itself to us, but how do we put this concept into practice? While true prayer is always open to the leading of the Spirit, we have found the following model faithful to the Reformed tradition and personally helpful. However, no model of prayer will ever express its full range of forms and meaning.

Meditate on the scriptures. Begin your prayer by listening for God to speak through the written Word. Relax and become quiet in God's presence. Read a passage from the gospels (for example, Matt. 5:1-14). Let God speak through the text; listen to it as God's word to you. In listening, a word or phrase or an idea often leaps from the text; turn that thought over in your mind, walk around it, listen to it. Repeat the word or phrase in rhythm with your breathing. Biblical meditation communicates God's word to us and prepares us to speak with God.

Praise God. Let your prayer to God begin with praise. Praise God for all that God means to you. Share your feelings of wonderment and awe as you sit in God's presence. The words of the psalmist are appropriate: "Praise the LORD, all you nations! Extol him, all you peoples! For great is his steadfast love toward us, and the faithfulness of the LORD endures forever. Praise the LORD!" (Psalm 117).

Make confession. Consider those things that block your communion with God. Reveal your life before the Searcher of the heart. Permit the Holy Spirit to bring to your consciousness the blocks between you and God. Confess your sins and receive forgiveness. Sin blocks prayer. Prayer without confession creates phony persons.

Give thanks. Review the blessings God has lavished upon you. Number them one by one. Verbally express your gratitude. When you cannot thank God "for" everything, you can thank God "in" everything.

Pray for others. Name those persons to God who need God's help. Intercession on their behalf evidences your love for your neighbors near and far. Pray for your family; pray for other members of the church; pray for government leaders;

remember the least and the lost of society; pray for your enemies.

Offer petitions. Make known your deepest desires. Ask God for the things you desire in your life; offer your prayers in the name of Jesus. These prayers will be according to the nature and the will of Christ. They are prayers he has already prayed.

Trust God. Commend your prayers to God with confidence that God has heard and will answer. When doubts come, recall the promises of Christ. The promises are true and faithful; God is our God and will not let us go. We have every right to believe that God is answering our prayer.

Pray "Our Father . . . " Conclude your prayer with the Lord's Prayer. It summarizes all you have prayed; it is the perfect prayer!

We commend this approach to prayer as a model that includes the essential elements of Reformed prayer. While it may not be vastly different from the way you have always prayed, we invite you to follow this pattern as a way of disciplined, effective prayer. To get started, set a time and place for a daily appointment with God. Such regular appointments are essential for living the Christian life with power and purpose.

God has provided still other means for our Christian growth. In the following chapter we see how scripture can also help us.

Questions for Reflection

1. How would you define prayer? What aspects of prayer does the Reformed tradition focus on?
2. What do you consider the greatest obstacles to consistent prayer?
3. How does public prayer relate to private prayer?
4. What is the role of scripture in prayer?
5. Do you consider your church a "praying church"?

5

Responding to Scripture as the Word of God

Peter had little to say when he came home from work on Wednesday evening. Mary knew something was troubling him, but she delayed bringing up the issue until after dinner. When they finished clearing away the dishes, and the kids had gone upstairs to begin their studies, she asked, "What's going on with you?"

"It's a conversation I had today at work," he responded.

"What was said?" she inquired.

"You know the Bible study group that meets an hour before work each Wednesday. Well, I had a confrontation with Jim Wright after the meeting today."

A little shocked, Mary asked, "What kind of confrontation?"

Peter then related how the group leader, Jim Wright, had asked the group what they thought about the Bible. Was it a human book or the inerrant Word of God? A few group members answered immediately, "The Bible is the Word of God!" Peter acknowledged his belief in the Bible as God's Word, but he was not sure about the term "inerrant."

When Peter voiced a question about the inerrancy of the Bible, Jim immediately took his response as a challenge to his leadership, authority, and integrity.

"Peter, are you one of those liberals who chooses what he wants to believe and cuts out the rest of the Bible?" Jim asked with a note of sarcasm in his voice.

"No. I don't think I'm that selective," Peter responded. "But I don't believe the Bible was written to give exact scientific data, for example." In this statement, Peter was thinking about the biblical account of creation or the sun standing still for Joshua.

"Well," Jim had countered "if you don't believe all of it, you might as well believe none of it!"

Recalling Sarah Makemie's discussion of the creeds and confessions of the church, Peter said, "My church believes the Bible is the authority for faith and practice of the Christian life, but not necessarily a scientific textbook. What we believe we express in creeds and confessions as a summary of biblical teaching."

His background being different, Jim Wright retorted, "I'm glad I belong to a church that has no creed but the Bible and no confession but Jesus Christ."

When Peter tried to respond to Jim's high-handed manner, Jim brushed him off and refused to discuss the matter. As a consequence, Peter had felt grief all day about his relationship with Jim. He was still depressed when he got home.

"What will you do?" asked Mary.

"I don't know," Peter said. "You know how much I have looked forward to the weekly studies. I have learned so much about the Bible, but I can't go along with Jim's dogmatism just to maintain acceptance in the group."

The issue raised by Peter's encounter with Jim Wright is commonplace in the modern church—how do we understand the authority of the Bible and its role in the life of the church and of the serious Christian? And how do we relate to persons in the church who hold the same views as Jim Wright? In this chapter we explore the historical nature of scripture, the role of scripture in the Reformed tradition, the necessity of the Holy Spirit in interpreting scripture, the appropriation of the teachings of scripture in our personal and corporate life, and the shape of a spirituality nurtured and formed by the word of God.

The Historical Character of the Bible

Contrary to the dogmatic affirmations of persons like Jim Wright, the Bible did not drop down from heaven in perfect form, untouched by human hands and unaffected by human history. Human involvement and contextual influences make the Bible an incarnational book—God's Word in human language—rather than an esoteric book of secret knowledge. Although Peter could not have explained the scriptures in this manner, he knew from his membership training that the Bible was both human and divine in origin.

Over several centuries, God made known the divine will to a people chosen for God's own purpose. God's action began with the call of Abraham (Gen. 12) and continued through the resurrection of Jesus Christ and the gift of the Holy Spirit. During these millennia, God acted in Israel's history, including the call of Abraham, Israel's bondage in Egypt, its deliverance through Moses, God's giving of the law, and Israel's taking possession of the land.

In these events Israel encountered God, and the memory and meaning of these encounters were conserved in narratives. These stories were repeated through the years, and the telling of the stories shaped Israel's character, nurtured Israel's faith, and pointed toward Israel's destiny. God spoke through the telling of the stories. As time passed, the stories were supplemented with hymns, poems, oracles, and prophecies.

Eventually these stories, hymns, poems, oracles, and prophecies were written. The written records became the sacred texts of the Hebrew people. The scriptures of the Old Testament are foundational for Christian faith.

The New Testament came into being in much the same way. Though its origin is much closer to us in time, it was written some nineteen hundred years ago. A series of events introduced Jesus Christ to the world. Stories about his birth, life, teaching, healings, death, and resurrection were preserved in the Christian community. Early on, some of his teachings, stories, healings, and miracles were written down. From these earliest sources, the gospel writers constructed the Synoptic Gospels—Matthew, Mark, and Luke, which see the life of Jesus similarly. The stories of Jesus were sermons or the basis for sermons in the first century much as they are today.

The book of The Acts of the Apostles tells of the coming of the Holy Spirit and the expansion of the church. Most of the remainder of the New Testament consists of letters written by Paul and other leaders in the Christian movement and deal with specific issues of faith and life in the early church. The book of Revelation describes the end of the church, the coming of the kingdom, and the fulfillment of God's purpose in creation.

When these texts were first written, they did not immediately become the New Testament. Leaders of the early church struggled for about three hundred years deciding exactly which gospels, letters, and other books should be included in the canon. In 367 c.e., the first listing of the books of the New Testament as it presently exists was drawn up by Athanasius, Bishop of Alexandria. Various church synods soon endorsed it, and since that time the New Testament as we have it has been the standard for Christian faith and life.

Because of the historical nature of scripture, God has spoken the Word in self-revelation through many voices in a variety of circumstances over thousands of years. The question which the church and Christians have always faced is, How do we hear God's Word through the written words of scripture?

This concern has given rise to numerous approaches to the interpretation of sacred texts—literal, allegorical, spiritual, and critical. The critical approach uses the same tools as those used in other studies of ancient texts. This approach has several branches: textual criticism, the comparison of differences in various texts; redaction criticism, the influence of the author and the situation on revisions of the text; literary criticism, the use of literary techniques for the study of stories, poetry, and oracles; historical criticism, the interpretation of texts according to the historical circumstances in which they originated. All these approaches seek to hear the word of God spoken through scripture.

Because of the historical nature of the Bible, the reader must consider the situation in which authors wrote, their intentions, and how their insights speak to us today. This informed approach to the text saves us from absurd statements about the Bible and guides us in our interpretation of its meaning for our lives today. So the basic questions we ask are: What does the text say? What did it mean to the original hearer? What does this text mean to us today? What will we do as an act of obedience?

Scripture as Authority

If the scriptures were written in another era, how are we to use them or be guided by them today? At the core of Reformed faith stands the affirmation of scripture.

Calvin held the Bible in highest esteem. He believed everything necessary for the guidance of our lives was contained in scripture: "For scripture is the school of the Holy Spirit, in which, as nothing is omitted that is both necessary and useful to know, so nothing is taught but what is expedient to know."[1]

Because of Calvin's influence, those in the Reformed tradition have always taken seriously the biblical witness. Every Reformed confession has underscored the authority of scripture to form our faith and direct our lives. Most recently *A Brief Statement of Faith* testifies that "the same Spirit who inspired the prophets and apostles rules our faith and life in Christ through scripture."[2]

And what do the scriptures principally teach? They teach us who God is, who we are, what sin is, how God restores us to a right relationship through Jesus Christ, and how we can have communion with one another and with Christ. This is an oversimplification perhaps, but these emphases touch on crucial biblical themes.

The law of God tells us about our duty to God. It states:

> I am the Lord your God . . . You shall have no other gods before me.
> You shall not make for yourself an idol. . . .
> You shall not make wrongful use of the name of the LORD your God, for the LORD will not acquit anyone who misuses his name.
> Remember the Sabbath day, and keep it holy. . . .
> Honor your father and your mother. . . .
> You shall not murder.
> You shall not commit adultery.
> You shall not steal.
> You shall not bear false witness against your neighbor.
> You shall not covet your neighbor's house . . . or anything that belongs to your neighbor.
>
> (Ex. 20:2–16, abbreviated)

This emphasis on the law of God contrasts with a spirituality that ignores the ethical dimensions of the Christian faith. Some have made the chief elements of spirituality the experience of ecstasy or the reception of God's gifts. This human-centered spirituality often neglects obedience to the divine law.

What does obedience to the law mean with regard to Christian spirituality? It gives substance to our relationship with God. For example, we put God first in our lives. God's will matters more than our own success, our power over other persons, or even our profit. This lifestyle flows from the command, "You shall have no other gods before me" (Ex. 20:3). Each command of God gives substance to our spirituality.

The Interpretation of Scripture

Having seen how the scriptures are the authority for our belief about God and our duty to God, we inquire further into how scripture nurtures the Christian life. The question has been posed, "How does God speak to us today?" The answer to this question must include the work of the Spirit in making the words in the text come to life in our hearts.

The truth of the Bible becomes personal through the action of the Holy Spirit. Calvin emphasized that the meaning of scripture can only be perceived by faith. God persuades the mind, and that persuasion results from the *testimonium spiritus sancti,* the testimony of the Holy Spirit. "The eternal word is of no avail unless animated by the power of the Spirit. . . . All power of action, then, resides in the Spirit himself, and thus all praise ought to be entirely referred to God alone."[3] Thus, the authority of scripture does not reside in a book but in an experience in which the truth of God is made personal through the action of the Holy Spirit.[4]

Although the Bible is the written Word of God, our reading it amounts to nothing apart from the Spirit's action. Scripture, like the womb of Mary, is barren until the Spirit moves upon it in the conception of the Christ. The Spirit moves upon our hearts as we read through the scriptures, and the truth of Christ is conceived in us. We are dependent upon the Spirit to convince our minds and move our hearts.

Scripture in Public Worship

When we discussed worship, we showed how scripture commands a central role in public worship, from the call to worship to the benediction. In our services we read from scripture, proclaim its message, and confess our understanding of it through a creed or confession. But unless we hear the Word of God as it is read, proclaimed, and confessed, the divine word will not bear fruit in our lives. We therefore must pray that the Holy Spirit will illumine us as we listen attentively and expectantly.

We listen to the word through preaching, a means we have

already singled out to have great significance in the Reformed tradition. The Larger Catechism says that

> the truth of God maketh the reading, but especially the preaching of the word, an effective means of enlightening, convincing, and humbling sinners, of driving them out of themselves and drawing them on to Christ, of conforming them to his image . . . of building them up in grace, and establishing their hearts in holiness and comfort through faith unto salvation.[5]

When we listen attentively to a sermon, praying for the Spirit to speak to us, the human word becomes a divine word. It stamps itself indelibly upon our hearts and calls us to obey. Recall the effect of Peter's sermon at Pentecost: when his audience heard the message, they were "cut to the heart" (Acts 2:37). Such is the case when the minister preaches in the power of the Spirit, and we pray for the Spirit to speak to us.

In public worship we have a responsibility to hear the proclaimed word of God; that is, "to discern Jesus Christ, to receive his offered grace, to respond to his call with obedience."[6]

What would happen if we prayed for a message from God each Sunday? What would happen if we prayed for the preacher as a spokesperson for God? What if we examined the sermon in the light of scripture? What if we received the truth with faith, love, meekness, and readiness of mind? What if we meditated upon it, hid it in our hearts, and lived it in our daily lives?

By affirming our faith through creeds and confessions in our worship, we also can hear God speak to us. The words we affirm are not magic, nor are they substitutes for scripture. Yet God can speak to us as we confess our faith through these summary statements of scripture. But again we must listen!

In all these ways we have identified—reading, proclaiming, confessing—scripture may inform our faith and shape our lives as followers of Jesus Christ. Scripture has been given as a means of grace to nurture us in the will of God. We do well to heed the words of Jesus, "Let anyone with ears listen!" (Matt. 13:9). Only as we hear responsibly in public worship can God use scripture as a means of grace. We receive nurture not just from the public hearing of the Word of God, however, but also in our personal worship.

Scripture in Personal Worship

The truth of the Bible also becomes personal for us in "secret" worship, as our tradition has often called it.[7] "Personal worship," says the Directory for Worship, "centers upon Scripture as one reads and listens for God's Spirit to speak."[8] We encourage using the scriptures in a variety of ways. Search them for guidance in making difficult decisions; read them for encouragement and comfort; get your marching orders from them.

Augment your reading with meditation. Meditation helps us hear God speak through scripture. Varieties of meditational practice abound from reflection upon a single word to the intellectual, reasoned system of Calvin. Meditation has content. It is not the rhythmic repetition of a mantra, nor a clearing of the mind of all thoughts, but rather a filling of the mind with God's holy history.[9]

Indeed, the Directory for Worship suggests a variety of methods of meditation on scripture, such as imaginatively entering into scripture. The Directory urges keeping a journal of insights and reflections, paraphrases, summaries, and positive decisions.[10] (See Ben Campbell Johnson's *To Pray God's Will* for additional suggestions.)

In personal worship as in public worship, earnestly pray for the Holy Spirit to illumine your mind that you may hear the word of God. One confession says, "God's word is spoken to his church today where the Scriptures are faithfully preached and attentively read in dependence on the illumination of the Holy Spirit and with readiness to receive their truth and direction."[11] The truth of the Bible becomes personal through the work of the Spirit, and prayer opens us to the Spirit, which makes us ready to receive the Spirit's direction.

Listen to the Word of God in family worship. Models and schedules from the past probably will not work today. Different schedules, different needs, and different ages and stages affect family worship. Even with these numerous obstacles, families who so desire can still incorporate the worship of God into their daily lives. At stake is our growth in faith and the transmission of our heritage to our children.

In the Reformed tradition we have always held that the Bible is a mirror that reflects the face of God, a scepter with which God governs, a staff with which God chastises, and an instrument of God's covenant made with us.[12] If the Bible is a mirror, a scepter, a staff, and the record of an alliance, we must give regular attention to its message so that it may transform our lives.

A Cluster of Resolutions

Scripture gives birth to, nurtures, and guides our spiritual development. Without the Word of God our spiritual life will perish. If the Bible holds such a central place as a means of grace, should not the serious disciple resolve to listen to its truth? Which of these resolutions seem appropriate for you?

In response to God's grace I resolve to

—attend public worship regularly with an intention to listen reverently to the reading and proclamation of the Word of God.

—pray that the text will be illumined by the Spirit in public worship and in my private reading.

—fix in my mind the condensed teachings of the scriptures by familiarizing myself with or memorizing the creeds and confessions of the church.

—recollect the meaning of the scriptural text during the week following public worship.

—engage in serious study of scripture in groups, classes, or private study for a deeper understanding of the will of God for the world and for my own life.

—keep a journal for personal responses to the insights gained from reading and meditating upon scripture.

—meditate on the text of scripture.

—explore different ways of listening to God through the study of scripture, for example, by copying sacred texts in my own handwriting and by memorizing, paraphrasing, and entering imaginatively into the text.

—read the Bible with my family.

As Peter read over a similar list of resolutions at First Church, he decided that he must do more than participate in the weekly Bible study before work. He checked off several resolutions he was willing to make, including reading the Bible with Mary. They bought their denomination's mission yearbook, which contained the lectionary readings for the day, prayers, and information about the work of their fellow Christians. By resolving to read it each day at bedtime, Peter and Mary opened their hearts for the Holy Spirit to speak to them.

Select the resolutions which best suit your personal needs and temperament and through them grow in knowledge of God's Word. Each of these resolutions aims to help us receive and respond to the grace of God mediated through scripture.

But God has provided still other means of grace for living the Christian life. We turn next to the sacraments and how they can strengthen us for discipleship.

Questions for Reflection

1. How did the Bible come into being?
2. In what sense is it the authority for faith and life?
3. What is the role of scripture in the worship of God?
4. How can your church help its members improve their understanding of the Bible?
5. What are several effective ways of personally studying the scriptures?

6

The Sacraments and a Vital Spirituality

"She's really done it this time," Hal Clarke was saying to his wife, Evelyn. Peter and Mary overheard the remark as they were coming out of their Sunday school class.

"What do you mean, Hal?" Peter inquired.

"Sarah Makemie has scheduled two baptisms and the Lord's Supper today."

"What's wrong with that?" Mary asked innocently.

"What's wrong? I'll tell you what's wrong! Every time we have Communion, the service runs an extra fifteen minutes, and I don't like the way these baptisms just show off the children, who nine times out of ten cry throughout the whole ordeal."

When Hal ended his tirade, Peter said, "After our training, Mary and I have a different view of the sacraments."

"That special meaning has not come to me," Hal was muttering as he turned down the hallway that led to the parking lot.

As Peter watched Hal and his wife disappear around the corner, he felt an urge to follow. The night before, he and Mary had attended the twentieth wedding anniversary of the Jensens, also members at First Presbyterian Church. At the party Peter had been drinking freely. The alcohol had impaired his judgment and caused him to drive erratically on his way home after the party. The next morning Peter was overcome with a sense of guilt when he remembered his behavior.

Peter's urge to follow Hal stemmed from his sense of failure as a Christian, not the issue of an extra fifteen minutes added to the service. Because of his shame, Peter resisted facing the Lord, much like another Peter, who denied his Lord.

As Peter reviewed his own failure, he could not help recalling that Hal Clarke had attended the same party. When Peter went to a bathroom upstairs, he had observed Hal embracing Martha Selkirk in the hallway. Both had seemed stunned when they realized they had been seen.

When Peter and Mary took their usual places in the sanctuary, Mary tugged at Peter's hand as if she had read his thoughts. "Don't you remember what Dr. Makemie said in the sermon of preparation last week? The sacraments are means of grace to renew our lives." As the organ prelude began, a picture of Christ on the cross came into Peter's mind. Accompanying the mental image came the words, "It was for you."

How many Christians fail to appreciate the power of the sacraments! Perhaps if we understood the meaning of the sacraments and how to appropriate their nurture in our lives, we would begin to experience these gifts of God as means of growth and not an unwelcome addition to the service of worship.

The Meaning of the Sacraments

The Reformed heritage strongly emphasizes the sacraments for faith and the life of faith. Calvin stressed them in his teaching: "We have in the sacraments another aid to our faith related to the preaching of the gospel."[1] Moreover, he said, "But as our faith is slight and feeble unless it be propped up on all sides and sustained by every means, it trembles, wavers, totters, and at last gives way."[2]

God "props up our faith" by confirming the promises of the gospel through the visible signs contained in baptism and the Lord's Supper. God further enhances our Christian growth within the church by means of the continual use of the Lord's Supper and baptism; we have the Word of God; we see, feel, taste, and touch the sacraments. These symbols speak at a depth and in ways which the Word alone does not.

Strong teaching? Yes! And in our common life we have shockingly neglected the sacraments, relegating them to a secondary place in our worship. How often we have observed baptism without renewing our own baptismal vows, without discerning the part God calls us to play in nurturing the one being baptized. At the baptism of an infant, we have been more interested in the baby's attire than in the deeper meaning of the sacrament administered. Or, in regard to the Lord's

Supper, we have observed it once a quarter in some of our churches, believing that more frequent observance would make the Supper less meaningful. Why do you suppose that Hal and Evelyn Clarke skipped the baptisms and the Holy Communion? Was it merely the few minutes added to the service? Or was it a lack of appreciation for the significance of the sacraments?

Not only have we neglected the sacraments, we have misunderstood them. Because of our confusion about baptism, for example, some have argued that we ought to observe baptism more than once. "If someone who was baptized as an infant wants to be re-baptized as an adult, then why not do it?" an elder asks. "After all, she had a deep Christian experience at that church conference." Presbyterians understand that baptism initiates a person into the covenant community, and further experiences of grace appropriate more fully the significance of baptism. Does not this genuine experience of grace legitimate an "enlightened" baptism?

Or how many times have we come to the Lord's Table without previously confessing our sins? Self-examination and repentance seemingly have little place in our Communion vocabulary. We thereby may "eat and drink judgment" upon ourselves, as Paul suggested to the Corinthian Christians (1 Cor. 11:29). We often resist being confronted by our sinfulness.

If our perspective on baptism and Communion is in error, we neglect and misunderstand two important means of grace given us for Christian growth. Realizing this, Reformed Christians need to reappropriate the significance of the sacraments for their life of faith. Would not such enlightenment help cure our neglect of this means of grace?

The Heidelberg Catechism states that sacraments are "visible, holy signs, and seals instituted by God in order that by their use he may the more fully disclose and seal to us the promises of the gospel."[3] Let us examine this definition.

Sacraments are *visible*. We can see the water, pick up the bread, taste the wine. What they represent, like the washing away of sins, is invisible. These visible reminders of God's promises show outwardly what happens inwardly.

Sacraments are *holy signs*. In a sacrament, God takes something that is common, like bread, and designates it for a holy use. The bread becomes a sign of something holy; it signifies or points to the body of Christ broken for us. The sign is not empty, bearing no connection to what it signifies. Rather, a relationship exists between the sign—the bread— and what it signifies—the body of Christ. Appropriately, at the Lord's Table we call bread the body of Christ. Reformed confessions are quick to point out that the elements "still remain bread and wine."[4]

Moreover, sacraments are *seals*. With respect to a sacrament, a seal signifies a guarantee. When a legal document requires a signature to be verified, we ask a notary public to stamp a seal on the document to guarantee our signature. Scripture contains God's promise; preaching interprets the scriptural promise; the sacraments function as seals, guaranteeing the promises proclaimed in scripture.

The sacraments are signs and seals of the *promises of the gospel.* And what are these promises? God's love for humankind in spite of our rebellion. God's forgiveness of our sins, as heinous as they may be. God's offer of new life in Christ, no matter how bad our past. Catherine Gonzalez has written, "It is this love and mercy, this faithfulness and constancy of God, that form the core of all God's promises to us."[5]

Baptism and the Lord's Supper as sacraments have much in common. Both sacraments

> come from God and are commended by Christ,
> focus on Christ and his benefits,
> are seals of the same covenant of grace,
> center in the death and resurrection of Christ,
> depend on the preaching of God's promises in scripture,
> call us to repentance,
> summon us to grow in the life of faith.[6]

The Lord's Supper and baptism are sacraments of the covenant of grace, and when enacted or considered the emphasis must fall on God's love! Faith is our response to that love. In baptism and the Lord's Supper the Reformed tradition stresses what God promises, not what we promise.

To realize what these sacraments signify, consider the death and resurrection of Jesus Christ; the promises of God that the sacraments seal are seen most clearly in these mighty acts. His death reveals the horror of sin and its result. Yet in "the one sacrifice of Christ accomplished on the cross he graciously grants us the forgiveness of sins and eternal life."[7] The resurrection declares the victory of God over the worst that sin could do. God raised Jesus from the dead, showing God's power over sin and death. So God promises love and mercy and new life to all of us in the midst of our sin and alienation. These are the promises God made, these are the promises God keeps. We proclaim these promises in preaching; we enact and seal these promises in the sacraments.

While there are similarities in the two sacraments, there are significant differences:

Baptism marks our incorporation into Christ and the church, while the Lord's Supper nourishes the relationship.

Baptism is administered only once, the Lord's Supper often.

Baptism, though also communal in character, has an individual aspect because the person baptized is named specifically.

Baptism precedes the Lord's Supper, for we go from the font to the Table, not the reverse.

Catherine Gonzalez says, "If baptism is engrafting into Christ, the Lord's Supper is the continuous nourishment from the root that any graft needs if it is to stay alive. Jesus is the vine, and we are the branches (John 15:5). Baptism is the sign and seal of the beginning of our new life in Christ. . . . Communion is the seal of the feeding of that new life."[8]

Suppose Hal Clarke had understood that baptism and the celebration of the Lord's Supper were visible, holy signs and seals of the Lord's promises in which he also participated. Would he have decided to skip worship that Sunday? Does he have no sins for which his baptism promises cleansing? Does he not need the nurture that comes from sitting at the Lord's Table?

Yet we cannot hold Hal Clarke entirely responsible for his failure to appreciate the nourishing power of the sacraments. Too many churches fail to celebrate baptism and the Lord's Supper with either sensitivity or regularity.

Having examined the meaning of the sacraments, their similarities and differences, and our different responses to them, we now look more deeply into the role of each in the shaping of a Reformed spirituality.

Baptism

Calvin has an appropriate admonition for the Hal Clarkes and Peter Simpsons of the church: "Therefore, as often as we fall away, we ought to recall the memory of our baptism and fortify our minds with it, that we may always be sure and confident of the forgiveness of sins. For though baptism, administered only once, seemed to have passed, it was still not destroyed by subsequent sins."[9] Let us look more closely at how baptism can be a means of grace for us.

Baptism suggests that we live in and for Jesus Christ. Calvin says: "Baptism is the sign of the initiation by which we are received into the society of the church, in order that, engrafted in Christ, we may be reckoned among God's children."[10] From his statement we immediately see that we are made partakers of Christ. The engrafting motif has been woven into the fabric of our heritage; it indicates that we are united with Christ, incorporated into him. If we are so incorporated into Christ, we participate in his death and resurrection. Paul put it this way: "Therefore we have been buried with him by baptism into death, so that, just as Christ was raised from the dead by the glory of the Father, so we too might walk in newness of life" (Rom. 6:4). Jesus has died our death for us—in baptism we die to our old nature. Jesus has been raised for us, so in baptism we are raised with him. As a consequence we live the new life that he promises us in the gospel.

But we also live in and for the church. Being incorporated into Christ is more than an individual relationship with Christ; it means being incorporated into his Body, the church. Calvin said, and the confessions also affirm, that baptism is the initiatory sign by which we are admitted into the fellowship of the church. If we are engrafted into Christ, then we are automatically united with all who believe in him. This fact explains why baptism has been seen as a sign of entrance into the church. Baptism seals the promise that we are engrafted into the body of Christ when we are baptized into Christ. Baptism unites and binds together all who believe in Jesus Christ.

Through our baptism we live in and for the world. Christ himself said, "Go therefore and make disciples of all nations, baptizing them . . . " (Matt. 28:19f.). "Baptism," states the Directory for Worship, "is God's gift of grace and also God's summons to respond to that grace. . . . Baptism gives the church its identity and commissions the church for ministry to the world."[11] Many of the baptismal motifs seem passive— something is done for us, such as having our sins washed away. This meaning of baptism, however, is active, something we do for the world. Indeed, the church exists for the world; we are priests in the world.

Almost a year had elapsed since Peter had joined the church and claimed the meaning of his baptism, which had been administered more than thirty-five years earlier. Later he came to personal faith in Jesus Christ. But after growing as a Christian since making his profession of faith, he failed himself and his Lord at the Jensens' party. His behavior reminded him of the way he had acted at fraternity parties. How could he regain a sense of forgiveness and the renewal of his faith?

Already he had prayed for God's forgiveness. He had also asked Mary's pardon. But he had come to see that his sin affected the whole body of Christ. That Sunday morning in the sacrament of baptism he, along with the whole church, would again claim the promise of Christ. As he rehearsed his intentions, he suddenly saw that every baptism should be a renewal of baptism for the whole congregation!

And the power of baptism follows us into life. Luther suggested to his followers that each morning upon arising, they place a hand upon the head where the water of the sacrament had been applied and say, "I am baptized."[12] So baptism not only deals with sins previously committed, but with sins committed during the rest of our lives. Baptism is a perpetual sign of God's forgiveness, a sign that we need to be renewed in faith often. Baptism can thus be claimed at special services for renewing our baptismal vows, or when a baby or an adult is baptized, or every morning as Luther suggested.

The Lord's Supper

What does it mean to partake of the bread and wine? How does this sacramental act nourish and inform our spirituality? For the Supper to have meaning for us, we must come to the Table in faith, believe Jesus Christ is present at the Supper, and realize we are joined with other Christians as we confess our sins and share the elements. As a result we will grow in the Christian life. The Supper becomes a powerful means of grace, a principal way God nurtures us.

We come to the Table in faith. Let us not forget that faith, faith inspired by the Spirit, is necessary for the Lord's Supper to be effective in our lives. It is true that the Supper is primarily a sacrament of grace, not faith. It is founded on the promises of God, not our promises. Yet does not grace have to be received? And received by faith? There is nothing magical about eating the bread and drinking the wine at Communion. The elements, as helpful as they can be, do not automatically convey the benefits of God's grace. As Calvin said, "They avail and profit nothing unless received in *faith*.[13]

So faith—our faith—is essential for the Supper to nourish us. Faith establishes our worthiness to receive the sacrament. But we must understand that "the worthiness which is commanded by God," wrote Calvin, "consists chiefly in faith, which reposes all things in Christ, but nothing in ourselves. . . . "[14] It is not our worthiness in ourselves that qualifies us to receive the sacrament, but rather the worthiness of Christ. If the Supper depended on our worthiness, we would never take part. We become worthy only as we realize that there is no worth in us, only in Christ.[15]

Can you not imagine Peter saying at Communion, "I feel too unworthy to receive the bread and wine today"?

And would not Dr. Makemie quickly respond, "This Supper is for those who feel unworthy, who are sorry for their sins. No one of us is worthy, only Christ. Take it, eat, it's for you."

By penitently approaching Communion that Sunday, Peter exhibited faith. He knew he was not worthy to receive the Lord's body and blood. By having faith in the worthiness of Christ, however, he could partake with confidence. When Dr. Makemie offered Peter the bread and wine, he eagerly ate and drank, renewing and strengthening his faith.

Jesus Christ is present at the Supper. Sometimes we have referred to the presence of Christ as his real presence, at other times as his true presence. Theologians have struggled to explain how Christ is present. And when we have exhausted our best efforts to define his presence, with Calvin we must speak of "the mystery of the Supper."[16] But it is not so mysterious that we cannot seek to understand it better!

The Westminster Confession of Faith states that spiritually we "receive and feed upon Christ crucified, and all benefits of his death. . . . "[17] Presbyterians have always believed that Christ is really present in the Supper, spiritually present. Christ is not bodily present in the elements as Roman Catholics believe, nor is he "in, with, and under the bread and wine," as Lutherans believe. But nonetheless Christ is present to our faith. How can we understand "present to our faith"?

Donald M. Baillie once explained spiritual presence in terms of a relationship. He said that we can never understand God's presence in terms of "local" or "spatial" presence. What is more helpful, he said, is to think of God's presence as a personal relationship that can transcend time and space. It therefore is a spiritual relationship.[18]

Following Baillie, we can see how the personal can become spiritual by doing a little exercise in imagination. All of us have had the experience of being separated from someone whom we know and love. By recalling their memory they can actually become present in our consciousness. The awareness of that person's "presence" may become more powerful than that of other people actually seated in a room with us. Memory transcends time and space. In the same way, Christ becomes present with us through our personal relationship with him. And the Supper may enable us to become more acutely aware of his presence.[19]

But we believe that Christ's presence is more than a memory at the Table. Though he is not bodily present, he is with us in the Spirit, penetrating us like the rays of the sun. As Calvin explained, the ascended Christ transcends us. So does the sun, yet its rays warm us, heal us, illumine us. As we join our fellow Christians at the Table, our faith, awakened by the Spirit, unites us with the ascended Christ. The Spirit makes available to us, like the rays of the sun, the warming, healing, forgiving power of Christ. When we touch, taste, eat, and drink the elements, they communicate the presence of Christ to us more than words possibly could.[20]

In the early church, however the mystery of the presence occurred, an attitude of expectancy pervaded their worship. According to Oscar Cullmann, the *maranatha* prayer, "Come, Lord," originated in the Communion liturgy. Imagine the believing community gathered about the Table chanting, "*Maranatha, maranatha, maranatha,*" expecting Christ to join them in the feast much as he did after the resurrection. (See Luke 24:36–44.) If we are expecting the presence of Christ at the Table, will we not be more likely to recognize his presence with us there?

We eat and drink together at the Lord's Table. The Lord's Supper is corporate in nature, not individualistic. In administering the Lord's Supper to the sick, the Directory for Worship states that the Supper "is not to be understood as a private ceremony or devotional exercise, but as an act of the whole church, which shall be represented not only by the minister . . . but also by one or more members of the congregation authorized by the session to represent the church."[21] This directive for administering the sacrament to the sick makes clear the communal nature of the Supper. Our tradition has always understood it to be a sacrament of the church, never purely an individual affair. Only through the Word of God and sacraments within the church does Jesus Christ meet us and offer us his healing, forgiving presence.

As a corporate act, the Lord's Supper celebrates the fellowship believers have not only with Christ but also with one another. The Larger Catechism says that believers "testify and renew . . . *their mutual love and fellowship with each other,* as members of the same mystical body."[22] We believe in fellowship with other believers so strongly that we do not participate in private celebrations of the Supper. Those with whom we weep and rejoice in the church must be present.

Often at First Church they sang after Communion: "Blest be the tie that binds our hearts in Christian love: The fellowship of kindred minds is like to that above."[23] Such fellowship transcends all distinctions of gender, race, class, or nation. And this fellowship the Reformed tradition has always appreciated, knowing that the Lord's Supper is a sacrament of the church.

We come to the Table, then, in faith; Jesus Christ is present at the Table; and we eat and drink together. And so the Lord's Supper helps us to grow in the Christian life. In baptism we are initiated into the church. In the Lord's Supper we eat the food which nourishes and sustains us in our journeys of faith. And the food is nothing less than the broken body and shed blood of Jesus Christ. Can we not be grateful to a God who provides for us so generously?

If the Lord's Supper is so crucial for our spiritual nurture, why do so many of us abstain? When we grow in our understanding that Christ presents himself to us in the bread and wine, offering us his mercy so badly needed, then no power on earth can keep us from the Table. Once we have truly eaten in his presence we will change our priorities.

Sacraments and Spirituality

What do sacraments reveal to us about a Reformed spirituality? First, we must acknowledge that Reformed spirituality has a strong communal foundation. Baptism immerses us in a community of believing people, the Supper nourishes us together in this community. A communal spirituality contrasts with a highly individualistic spirituality, a "Jesus-and-me" perspective. Perhaps this explains why services of rededication, altar calls, or special prayer for spiritual healing do not find a regular place in most Presbyterian services. While these practices deepen spiritual life in certain "free church" communities, Presbyterians have drawn strength from the efficacy of baptism and the nurture of the Lord's Supper.

This description of the role of the sacraments in spiritual growth further underscores the lack of knowledge we have of these means of grace. Imagine what new life our congregations would experience if all of us took our place with Christ at each baptism and had fellowship with him at every Supper.

A Reformed spirituality, furthermore, rests in the grace of God, not in human efforts. Nothing makes this point more clearly than the sacraments. We do not receive them because we are worthy; we do not retain their benefits by our own efforts. In this grace, a Reformed spirituality has freedom from self-effort and from a "bad conscience," so that with joy and abandonment believing Christians may pursue the will of God.

Questions for Reflection

1. What is a sacrament?
2. How many sacraments do Reformed churches recognize? Upon what events in the life of Jesus are they based?
3. In what ways are the sacraments spiritually formative? Spiritually nourishing?
4. How do you evaluate the administration and celebration of the sacraments in your congregation?
5. What changes would make the reception of the sacraments more meaningful to you?

CHALLENGES
OF THE
CHRISTIAN LIFE

7

Spirituality Requires
Self-Denial

Peter and Mary, members of First Church for over a year, took seriously their decision to join the church and used the available means of grace to deepen their faith and their commitment. They did not realize how well God was preparing them for new, life-changing challenges.

For a couple of months, they participated in an adult Sunday school class that was struggling with major issues confronting contemporary society. They were challenged to look at the roots of our consumer culture, its values, the conversion of resources in the production of goods, the economic exploitation of poorer countries, the fact that with 6 percent of the world's population our country consumes well over 40 percent of the world's available resources.

To connect this lust for goods to the exploitation of the poor took little imagination, and Peter and Mary realized that U.S. business investments abroad figured directly into U.S. foreign policy and the threat of military intervention.

On the way home from worship, Mary asked, "Peter, what difference do you think the things we are learning should make in the way we live our lives?"

"I'm not sure," responded Peter, "but our life of faith cannot be lived in isolation from these pressing issues of our time."

Mary said, "I think we could begin to find an answer if we looked more deeply into the tradition of faith into which we've been baptized."

Peter and Mary had been thrust into a struggle involving the meaning of their faith in the context of social, political, and moral issues facing the church. Their questions about lifestyle and personal involvement weighed heavily upon them. Fortunately, they became part of a church that has a history of applying Christian commitment to crucial social issues. With respect to how life is to be lived, John Calvin emphasized that a Christian's whole life is but one act of repentance, and the discipline required consists of three parts: self-denial, cross bearing, and meditation on the future life. Ronald S. Wallace described it thus: "Involved in the doctrine of repentance, Calvin finds a 'rule for holy living.' This rule consists of three continuous exercises: self-denial, the mortification of the flesh, and meditating upon the heavenly life."[1] In more contemporary language these challenges may be referred to as living for Christ and others, not for ourselves; taking up the pain and suffering of the world and accepting our own; evaluating the present in the perspective of eternity. These challenges in the Christian life must not be looked upon as meritorious but as an opportunity to "turn" toward God. In successive chapters, we will examine each of these disciplines as they shape the Christian life.

Self-Denial

Self-denial makes room for the unreserved dedication of oneself. But the importance of self-denial will be missed unless it is placed in the context of human fallenness and sinfulness. Given the distortion of our nature, there is no limit to the excesses of our unrestrained desires. In the process of self-denial, however, the minds of believing persons can be transformed.

Calvin calls us to live a transformed life. He urges: "We are not our own, we are God's."[2] God has graciously given us the scriptures to guide our lives and has been explicit in calling us to complete dedication. Paul writes,

> I appeal to you therefore, brothers and sisters, by the mercies of God, to present your bodies as a living sacrifice, holy and acceptable to God, which is your spiritual worship. Do not be conformed to this world, but be transformed by the renewing of your minds, so that you may discern what is the will of God— what is good and acceptable and perfect. (Rom. 12:1-2)

This admonition calls us to present ourselves to God as a sacrifice. No longer is the offering the bleeding animal upon the altar, but our own lives. Dedication to God requires first the denial of our own will. This denial aspect Jesus made clear to his disciples when he said, "If any want to become my followers, let them deny themselves and take up their cross and follow me. For those who want to save their life will lose it, and those who lose their life for my sake, and for the sake of the gospel, will save it" (Mark 8:34–35).

But we must understand why self-denial is so necessary for us as Christians. Already we have seen how the fall of Adam corrupted all persons. Calvin believed that in the Fall the human heart not only has been corrupted but also has become possessed by an active principle or law of sin called "concupiscence."[3] Concupiscence appears in human consciousness as an active power that allures the mind and entices the will toward temporal, if not base, fulfillments. When the first pair and all their offspring rejected God as the sovereign Lord and the fulfillment of their lives, this undisciplined urge turned toward the material world to find fulfillment. Bereft of God, the soul is left to its own perverse urges. Concupiscence cannot be identified with mere lust or evil desire or appetite—it is rather what brings forth evil desire itself.[4] To be whole we need healing for this "disease" of concupiscence, which pushes us toward self-centeredness and away from the claims and fellowship of God and our neighbor.

Here enters the necessity for self-denial for Calvin. All of us fight an inner battle with this self-centered perversion. Self-denial for Calvin meant more than self-control; it meant a crucifixion in which God puts to death our old nature and gives us a new nature in Christ. Nothing less will cure the devastation of concupiscence. So by faith we consent to the crucifixion of our old nature.[5] God has chosen to heal us through the death of Christ. We die with Christ on the cross; we are raised to new life with Christ in the resurrection. God gives us new affections and powers; we are new creations. And it is God's Holy Spirit who makes the new creation possible through the benefits of the death of Christ.[6]

Let no one think that the battle ends with the creation of new life. Calvin surely did not, and neither do we. He described the Christian life as a battle with our old nature whose "affections and impulses tend always to lead us astray."[7] After the word of God has laid claim upon our minds and hearts, through self-denial we strive to subdue the unruly thoughts and passions that arise. Even when we yield ourselves to God's Spirit, we never achieve a perfectly harmonious unity with God's will.[8] Rather, the more control God gains over us, the more we have to deny our perverse natural inclinations, which rebel against the will of God.

In a way that repels the modern mentality, Calvin said that Christians must learn to hate themselves. To him self-denial meant a substitution of self-hatred for self-love. Self-love causes us to "despise and neglect others—produces cruelty, covetousness, violence, deceit, and all the kindred vices, and arms us with the desire of revenge."[9] We cannot wholly agree with our mentor, but the point he seeks to establish is valid— the sinful self must die. But we have come to believe that those who hate themselves hate others. Those persons who refuse to face their own depths of fear and self-rejection project their self-hatred onto others. If we hate ourselves, we will hate others; if we learn to love ourselves truly, we may learn to love others. This positive self-love arises when we know that we are accepted in spite of our sin and are loved unconditionally. Perhaps this positive love arises beyond the death of selfish desires.

Possibly we can reinterpret Calvin's radical "hate" of the self through the love of Christ. Even when we were sinners and had pushed God out of our lives, Christ loved us and died for us. By faith we are crucified with him, and the Holy Spirit pours God's love into our hearts. Being so richly loved by God leads us to an appropriate self-love and a genuine love for our neighbor. Though our battle never ends, we can develop a healthy love of self.

Let us not forget that no matter how much we grow, the old passions still surge in our hearts: the temptation to wealth, the love of influence, the lust for power. Calvin says,

> Scripture calls us to resign ourselves and all our possessions to the Lord's will, and to yield to him the desires of our hearts to be tamed and subjugated. To covet wealth and honors, to strive for authority, to heap up riches, to gather together all those follies which seem to make for magnificence and pomp, our lust is mad, our desire endless.[10]

The rule of self-denial must be applied to all these perverse, rebellious desires.

The challenge to get control of the self has several obstacles: unruly thoughts, our own unaided judgment, undisciplined passions, self-idolization. At the core of these perversions lies the substitution of the self for God. Humans tend to look to their own rationalizations to order their lives rather than to the Word of God. But human reason has been so perverted that it leads like a blind guide who lands us constantly in the ditch. Even if reason were clear enough to conceive the highest good for us, our will lacks the steadfastness to do what is good. Like Paul, we too confess, "I do not understand my own actions. For I do not do what I want, but I do the very thing I hate" (Rom. 7:15). Thus, God calls us to deny ourselves that we may dedicate our whole being to the service of God.[11]

This insidious and progressive power of concupiscence unfolds its plot in gentle, persuasive steps. In the first stage of temptation a fantasy flutters through the mind stimulated either by some external object or internal urge. As the fantasy gains energy, it takes clearer and sharper form until the vision becomes as real as if the temptation were literally there. With the object of desire so clearly conceived, it enters the will and wins consent. This inward "yes" releases all of the power of the mind and body to fulfill itself through indulgence. And this external act climaxes the intent of human concupiscence.

Concupiscence as we have described it gives birth to addiction. Addiction is the attachment of desire to anything less than God, and the sure evidence of addiction is seen in one's inability to deny oneself the fulfillment or pseudo-fulfillment addiction promises.

Whatever the addiction—drugs, alcohol, nicotine, caffeine, money, or food—it has destructive consequences. Addictions by definition enslave the will, but they do more. Addictions erode self-esteem, endanger health, impair functioning, and eventually kill.

From a spiritual perspective addictions provide substitutes for God; they provide new centers of attachment, fill the mind with obsessions and corrupt behavior that even when hated become irresistible.

The cure for addiction lies clearly in self-denial. By the grace of God, we say "no" to the power of concupiscence, no to our obsessions, no to our compulsions. Whatever treatment is required for our healing, at the core will be a rejection of the instant and repeated gratification of the undisciplined desires inspired by concupiscence.

In addition to healing addiction, self-denial has another

implication. Without much effort, we can see how commercial advertising stimulates the imagination, stirs desires, and overcomes the will in order to produce a sale. When the promised result has only a temporary effect, satisfying the desire soon becomes a habit and must be repeated again and again.

The desire for more and more things (concupiscence knows no rest; it cannot be silenced through satiation, only strengthened) feeds the mills of production, which must create more, new, and different products lest consumers become bored with repetition. The production of these products, which may be desired but not needed, consumes more and more resources, often for luxuries at a time when millions lack the necessities of life. Not all creation and production can be labeled evil; we do need to provide for life's necessities, and even the manufacture of luxury items provides jobs for workers and pleasures for many of us. But this minimal good does not offset the waste of resources, nor the value system it implies.

Though these consequences are serious enough, the tale of the snake does not end here. When the resources of labor and material have been exploited in one area, or when the price of production exceeds the limits of profitability, production shifts to another environment where raw materials are plentiful and labor cheaper. This move provides the backdrop for the exploitation of weaker countries and poorer peoples. What shame we must feel when we realize that some of our affluence has been won by riding on the backs of the poor.

When heavy investments have been made in plants and equipment, they must be protected at all costs. The concern over capital rises high enough when investments are made in dry goods and electronics, but when they involve oil or uranium, the stakes increase tenfold. Political unrest, stimulated by either economic injustice or political destabilization, becomes a factor, and a change of foreign policy or military intervention follows. National unrest threatens the capital investment and the flow of goods to feed the concupiscence of the powerful.

Depending on the depth of the unrest and the severity of conflict, the specter of sanctions or war looms on the horizon. If the conflict involves the superpowers of the world, the threat of nuclear holocaust hangs like a cosmic eraser over humankind.

All this from concupiscence, which excites evil desires and lust in our hearts.

Self-Denial in World Context

In the context of a consumer society that values material goods and sensual delights, we are faced with the call to deny materialism's control over our lives. Perhaps Paul's letter to Titus offers necessary guidance:

> For the grace of God has appeared, bringing salvation to all, training us to renounce impiety and worldly passions, and in the present age to live lives that are self-controlled, upright, and godly, while we wait for the blessed hope and the manifestation of the glory of our great God and Savior, Jesus Christ. He it is who gave himself for us that he might redeem us from all inequity and purify for himself a people of his own who are zealous for good deeds. (Titus 2:11–14)

According to this text, self-denial includes the rejection of ungodliness, worldly desire, and passions of the flesh. To renounce ungodliness calls us to turn from whatever is not like God. God graciously created us, sharing the very image of godself with us. This self-giving love stands in stark contradiction to every form of self-seeking greed as well as every addiction.

The rejection of worldly desire calls for new values and goals. The drive for success, ambition, the lust for power, and the demand for control—all these give way to freedom, companionship, and partnership. This changes the arrangement of where we perceive God—from "above" to "beside" us.

Self-denial also includes the discipline of the passions. Desire stimulated by fantasy must be brought into submission to Christ, who resisted every suggestion of the tempter to food, power, and vanity. (See Matt. 4:1–11.)

Do we not see that this rejection of the self as center of the world holds powerful implications for personal and interpersonal as well as international relations? At the personal level each of us is bound into a system of consumption: get, use, enjoy; but we have a choice about lifestyle and values. The values of American society drive us toward greed for material goods, fleshly pleasures, and worldly power and honor. All these lusts provide the motivation for our addictions.

What does self-denial mean in this sort of world? According to Calvin, it is necessary that a person "depart from himself in order that he may apply the whole force of his ability in the service of the Lord."[12] As we have seen, self-denial leads to dedication of one's life and the transformation of one's mind to divine service. In a sense, this transformation reverses the vision out of which the culturally conditioned man or woman lives.

Calvin identifies four aspects of a transformed mind—esteem of the other, helpfulness to the other, a vision of God in them, and an attitude of cheerfulness.[13] In accordance with scripture, we are to "regard others as better than [ourselves]" (Phil. 2:3). This attitude relieves us of competitiveness, one-up-manship, and using others for our advancement. What difference would it make in the corporate structure if each employee valued and respected the gifts of fellow workers? Would not numerous conflicts be overcome in families if this attitude prevailed? Is it not the discounting of our fellow human beings that ignites anger and supports a competitive environment? If respect for our fellows were extended to the workers in the fields or the laborers in the mills of Third World countries, would that not ease tensions in the world community?

But a transformed mind goes beyond mere respect; it actually seeks the welfare of the neighbor. How difficult it would be to seek wholeheartedly the good of our neighbor if we cling to our own rights and prerogatives. Calvin has it that our helpfulness consists of our "liberal and kindly sharing" of benefits with others.[14] Whatever God has so graciously given us must be used to help our neighbor. "Who is my neighbor?" The circle of neighbors includes all those who have need. So the transformed mind asks, "How can I assist my neighbor?" Not, "How can I use my neighbor?"

This way of relating to our fellow human beings springs not from their deserving our love but from their bearing the image of God. According to Calvin, "we are not to consider that men merit of themselves, but to look upon the image of God in all men, to which we owe all honor and love."[15] How can we abuse and exploit one who bears the image of God? Even if persons live in ways that offend our deepest sensitivities, we still owe them respect and helpfulness because they are made in the image of God.

This transformation of mind not only involves our behavior toward the neighbor who bears God's image, it also includes the *spirit* in which we relate to the neighbor. God will have no service born of duty or necessity, but from a "sincere feeling of love." When we know of others' ill fortune, we must put ourselves into their place and experience with them their pain and deprivation, that is, stand in solidarity with those who suffer. Surely this neighborliness includes those next to us, but it also reaches to the homeless, the unemployed, and the marginalized in our society. Yet the definition of neighbor cannot be confined even to those geographically near us. Is not the black of South Africa, or the native villager of Central America, or the citizen of Hungary also a neighbor who bears the image of God and demands our respect and helpfulness? In national and corporate relations, as well as close, interpersonal ones, self-denial is a prerequisite for love of neighbor.

Commitment to God

How can persons find the energy to resist the societal values, the comfort and self-indulgence that dominate society? What faith structure and what power beyond our own can we claim for this life of humble obedience? Perhaps we should first of all be reminded that Jesus Christ showed us the way. The Philippian hymn sings,

> Though he was in the form of God,
>   [he] did not regard equality with God
>   as something to be exploited,
> but emptied himself,
>   taking the form of a slave,
>   being born in human likeness.
> And being found in human form,
>   he humbled himself
>   and became obedient to the point of death—
>   even death on a cross.
>
> (Phil. 2:6–8)

Christ demonstrated the ultimate self-denial and revealed the ultimate in solidarity.

But for us who have been trapped in a false value system, mesmerized by the neon lights of human splendor, and gorged on consumption, the death of Christ and our participation in it provides a liberating power. Ronald S. Wallace, interpreting Calvin, reminds us that the death of Christ, more than a historic memory, is "a living force which men can encounter as a present, powerful, concrete factor in the shaping of their character and destiny."[16]

Our baptism marks our birthright in this new order. "Do

you not know," asks Paul, "that all of us who have been baptized into Christ Jesus were baptized into his death?" (Rom. 6:3). On the basis of our baptism, we can confidently claim freedom from the bondage of the past and a new power to "walk in newness of life" (Rom. 6:4). So there is hope for us who have lived in bondage to selfish, ungodly practices, worldly desires, and the passions of the flesh. In Jesus Christ, we have been liberated in order that we may choose an alternative lifestyle expressive of Christ. In moments when the battle with perverse desire rages, let us confidently claim the power of our baptism.

The crucifixion of our old, sinful self and our participation in the crucifixion through baptism finds an experiential reality in the ministry of the Holy Spirit. The Holy Spirit, the promised presence of Christ, becomes contemporary with us to effect in us all that our Lord's death and resurrection did for us. One side of self-denial requires renunciation of our sinful desires and practices, but the other side requires a demonstration of freedom and love for our neighbor through the power of the Holy Spirit. A resurrection of freedom inspired and bestowed by the Spirit means death to our enslavement to sin. Paul reminds the Galatians: "For you were called to freedom, brothers and sisters, only do not use your freedom as an opportunity for self-indulgence, but through love become slaves to one another" (Gal. 5:13). Could it be that this kind of freedom can empower us to envision an alternative world, one shaped by the cross and resurrection of our Lord, the ultimate paradigm for all our self-denial?

Beyond Self-Denial

At the outset, we affirmed that self-denial prepared the way for a larger vision of life, an alternative to a self-centered existence. The reconstruction of one's style of life may begin at the very intimate point of relations in the family, work, or church. In these three spheres, Calvin's admonition to respect others, show helpfulness, and be cheerful certainly applies. On the other hand, self-denial may be cast in the larger arena of consumerism, public policy, and care for the environment. As we have seen, these concerns may be distinguished, but not separated. One flows into and affects another. Regardless of the starting point, it would be important for a disciple of Jesus to begin consideration of a "new earth" vision, the creation of a supportive community, a shared covenant, and a renewed emphasis on stewardship.

A New Earth Vision. Most of us in the United States have either unconsciously or intentionally bought into a consumer-oriented, materialistic value system. A direct line of cause and effect may be drawn from consumerism to militarism and war. Personal lifestyle and world peace, therefore, cannot be separated no matter how unrelated they may seem. If we have been lured into a view of the world as a place for human consumption, rather than a mirror of God's glory, we must begin to construct a "new earth" vision.

If, instead of surrendering to every desire for "more," we began to live with the affirmation of "enough," would the result be a different vision of the earth? Instead of seeking more for ourselves, why do we not seek enough land for all to have a place, enough food for all to eat, enough work for all to have a job, enough value in humanity for every person to receive respect? If there is enough for all, there will be no shortages, unless some persons or groups begin to amass not only their share but that of others. Self-denial in this new earth vision means to renounce one's greed and refuse to take what rightfully belongs to another.

A Supportive Community. To begin changing our basic orientation toward life offers a challenge too great to undertake alone. Without the support of fellow Christians, with whom we may share our dreams and commitments, we likely will become discouraged. Weary from the struggle, we will be swallowed by the powerful rush of the materialistic tide. Just as Peter and Mary found support and encouragement at First Church, all of us need a community in which to be nurtured and strengthened.

We need support, but also accountability. Which of us in a moment of insight has not made noble decisions—to protect significant relationships, to seek a simpler lifestyle, or to challenge the values of the society? Yet when we are left to ourselves, good decisions seriously made may come to naught because of a lack of power to follow through. A supportive community not only holds us accountable but speaks the word of forgiveness when we fail in our high intentions.

While the church community gives support and accountability, the person beginning a new lifestyle will profit from a specific covenant. Because of the enormity of the challenge, a covenant keeps the central issues alive. One such covenant is as follows:

The Shakertown Pledge

Recognizing that the earth and the fulness thereof is a gift from our gracious God, and that we are called to cherish, nurture, and provide loving stewardship for the earth's resources,

And recognizing that life itself is a gift, and a call to responsibility, joy, and celebration,

I make the following declarations:

1. I declare myself to be a world citizen.
2. I commit myself to lead an ecologically sound life.
3. I commit myself to lead a life of creative simplicity and to share my personal wealth with the world's poor.
4. I commit myself to join with others in reshaping institutions in order to bring about a more just global society in which each person has full access to the needed resources for their physical, emotional, intellectual, and spiritual growth.
5. I commit myself to occupational accountability, and in so doing I will seek to avoid the creation of products which cause harm to others.
6. I affirm the gift of my body, and commit myself to its proper nourishment and physical well-being.
7. I commit myself to examine continually my relations with others, and to attempt to relate honestly, morally, and lovingly to those around me.
8. I commit myself to personal renewal through prayer, meditation, and study.
9. I commit myself to responsible participation in a community of faith.[17]

The earth, life, and all we have are gifts from a gracious God. They are "trusts," as Calvin put it. "Thus, therefore, we must so arrange it that this saying may continually resound in our ears: 'Render account of your stewardship.' "[18] God is Creator, and we are stewards of God's creation. We are not owners, only managers of God's world. Viewed from the perspective of stewardship, self-denial frees and empowers us to decide on actions for the common good: the protection of the environment from pollution, the control of carbon produced from burning fossil fuels, the banning of nuclear proliferation until means of disposal of nuclear waste can be found, the rejection of nuclear arms as a deterrent to war or in a full-fledged, hostile engagement.

If the mission of the church calls for our proactive engagement in resolving the issues before us, stewardship provides for the active care of the creation and the conditions that make life possible and desirable. Once aware of our plight, how many of us will discover "something" within ourselves which approves of the status quo and seeks its own way?

Questions for Reflection

1. What is meant by self-denial?
2. Why do Christians deny themselves?
3. What does self-denial mean in terms of our common life?
4. What is the relationship of self-denial to Christian spirituality?
5. How can your church guide and support its members in the discipline of self-denial?

8

Cross Bearing as a Form of Spirituality

What does it mean when Christians suffer? How are they to respond to calamity? How do they relate adverse occurrences to the will of God?

These were the questions that plagued Peter and Mary when adversity struck them. They had been members of First Church for two years. In that time they had begun to deepen their knowledge of scripture, prayer, the sacraments and worship; and they had made significant changes in their vocational goals, their spending, and their feeling of participation in the worldwide community of God. Little by little, they had begun to understand these changes as the type of spirituality Dr. Makemie had described in the new member class—an intelligent dedication to God.

Without warning, the shock came. One evening, while dressing for sleep, Mary felt a small, hard lump in her breast. She told Peter. He said, "It probably is nothing, but you had better have Dr. Washburn check it."

It took a week to get an appointment. She called Peter when she got the report: "Dr. Washburn says the test has come back positive, and she has scheduled surgery for me next week."

Peter hung up the phone. He thought, "Cancer? Surgery? What will happen to Mary?"

The surgery went well, and the doctor assured them that the medical team had "gotten all of it." After a few weeks of radiation treatments as a precaution, she should have no further difficulty from the cancer.

On the way home, Peter wondered aloud, "What is the Lord trying to teach us through this experience?"

"Do you think God is punishing us in some way?" Mary asked. "I'll be honest with you. The night before I went into surgery, I looked back over my life to see if God was trying to tell me something."

"Does God do that sort of thing?" asked Peter.

Their lives had barely settled into normalcy when Peter got a memorandum from the new chief executive officer at Addison, the engineering firm where he was working.

Little did Peter realize the consequences of the appointment with Jack Pederson. Jack called him into his office, and after a few minutes of informal conversation, he said, "I regret to inform you, Peter, that our profits have been down significantly, the volume of work has dried up, and your job is being eliminated. You have rendered valuable service to the company, and we are providing a year's severance pay."

Peter called Mary at her office to report the news to her. "I'll bring home a pizza for dinner. Let's get the kids to bed early so that we can talk. I have some heavy feelings I need to get out."

"I think this is the kind of experience that drives us to pray. Let's find some time to bring our feelings and needs before God," Mary responded.

After dinner, when the children had gone to their rooms, they sat quietly in the living room. Only then did Mary ask, "How did you feel when the conversation was over with your boss?"

"I felt stunned, I suppose. I just wasn't expecting this. In some ways, I feel afraid. What of my reputation, the future? It's embarrassing. And most of all I wonder where God is in all the things that have happened to us the past few months."

Mary's question had opened up the whole problem, and she and Peter talked together until early the next morning. Before retiring they committed themselves and their anxiety to God, asking for discernment as to what Peter's dismissal might mean in their lives.

The next Sunday, as worship began, Dr. Makemie read the text:

> Then Jesus told his disciples, "If any want to become my followers, let them deny themselves and take up their cross and follow me. For those who want to save their life will lose it, and those who lose their life for my sake will find it. For what will it profit them if they gain the whole world but forfeit their life? Or what will they give in return for their life?"
>
> (Matt. 16:24–26)

Peter's mind got stuck on verse 24: "If any want to become my followers, let them deny themselves and take up their cross and follow me." He began to wonder, "What is the relation of Mary's surgery and my job loss to carrying the cross?"

The Meaning of Cross Bearing

The scriptures make emphatic statements about disciples bearing the cross of Jesus. "Whoever does not carry the cross and follow me cannot be my disciple" (Luke 14:27). In some sense, Jesus bore the cross throughout his life. He was born with its prospect before him, lived in its shadow, and literally had it thrust upon his shoulders.

Yet the physical transport of crossed pieces of wood does not define "cross bearing." We have a friend who on Good Friday used to strip off his shirt, don jeans and sandals, place a huge, rustic cross on his naked shoulders, and carry it down Michigan Avenue to Chicago's Loop. A few spectators wondered, others sought to ignore him, still others asked, "Why?" Why the literal bearing of the cross? What significance, what statement was he trying to make?

Could it be that the drafting of Simon of Cyrene to carry Jesus' cross suggests a model? The scripture states, "As they led him away, they seized a man, Simon of Cyrene, who was coming from the country, and they laid the cross on him, and made him carry it behind Jesus" (Luke 23:26). This incident illustrates at least one aspect of cross bearing—in some sense our crosses are an aspect of his cross. Barth says of our cross, "It is clear that this cross stands in the closest relationship to that of Jesus Christ himself. The cross is the most concrete form of the fellowship between Christ and the Christian."[1] Yet he goes on to point out that the cross of the Christian relates only indirectly to the cross of Christ because his was one of suffering rejection for all humanity. Still, the crosses laid upon us are never meaningless calamities, unrelated to God's will for us. Like Christ's cross, they are instruments of God's will.

Our crosses are those occurrences in our lives which interrupt our plans, test our faith, and teach us patience in suffering. Barth identifies these crosses as misfortunes, accidents, sickness and age, parting from those most dearly loved, disruption, and even hostility in important human relations. He also includes slights and intentional and unintentional humiliations in his definition of the crosses we must bear.[2]

A few illustrations to clarify the point: A nurse on a late-night shift felt a call from God to adopt a terribly deformed child. She willingly adopted him, knowing that he would have five major reconstructive operations—is that embracing a cross?

A professor of finance begins going blind at age fifty-five and in three years is forced to retire—a cross?

Peter and Mary—an illness and a job loss—crosses?

Crosses like these do come to us, and how we respond to them gives shape and substance to our spirituality.

Cross Bearing and Providence

If we are to assist Peter and Mary with their questions about their recent experiences, we must connect the crosses they bear with the providence of God. In what way does cancer or a job loss relate to God?

John Calvin makes his position clear: "At the outset, let my readers grasp that providence means not that by which God idly observes from heaven what takes place on earth, but that by which as keeper of the keys, he governs all events."[3] The emphasis for Calvin falls on "governs"; God purposes and fulfills the divine will.

How then will we look upon the calamitous occurrences in our lives? Perhaps the middle ground rejected by Calvin, which has human freedom and responsibility mixed with divine sovereignty, offers a better place to stand. While some in the Reformed tradition might judge our attempt to understand God's sovereign will a distortion, we find it helpful to think of God's will in several aspects: *primal, provisional, permissive, and perfect.*[4] God's primal will, for example, intended complete obedience from the original pair. If we can conceive of a world without sin, we can envision that God truly desired trust and obedience from all.

Apparently God chose to risk human freedom and the perverse acts of the first humans, thereby exposing the creation to the invasion of chaos. In this new situation of creation mixed with chaos, God's provisional will entered. In this aspect, God provides the energy for creation to continue and space for human initiative and creativity. Yet, in this provision, God's ultimate intention for creation and all creatures will be realized.

In the present situation of creation and chaos, God permits evil to befall all creatures. All of us are implicated in the Fall; we bear responsibility and the consequences of "fallenness." So those calamitous consequences that seem evil arise from the imperfection of our being and the chaos that has invaded the creation. All these corruptions of God's primal will have occurred by divine permission, a view sometimes alluded to by Calvin. When we consider Mary's cancer, the fragility of her body and its lack of perfection created the possibility of cancer. It could not have come into being apart from the energy of God, which created and sustained her body. Nor could it have been without God's permission.

Finally, God wills ultimately the perfection of nature, society, and persons. In the time between the fall of creation and its final restoration, we participate in God's redemptive drama. In a broken world we look to the fulfillment of the promise of Christ—a new heaven and a new earth. Because of his promise of the future, we have hope. No matter what befalls us by way of illness or tragedy, we live with the assurance that God will fulfill the promise made in Christ.

With these distinctions in God's will, Peter and Mary can recognize that their lives, like those of others, have not progressed according to the primal intention of God. In God's provisional will, the creation of the body is vulnerable to the attack of sin and chaos that pervert and disrupt it. And God who continues the creation permits the destructive presence of cancer. God does not forsake Mary, but empowers her and gives her faith and hope. With confidence, Mary can look at the new heaven and new earth and the ultimate fulfillment of her body.

Why Our Crosses?

Whether these burdens and disruptions come to us by the intentional or permissive will of God, we struggle with the question of what the purpose might be for which these crosses fall upon our shoulders? Calvin proposes three reasons for the crosses in our lives: discipline, chastisement, persecution.

First, crosses have been given to discipline us, that is, to teach us. John H. Leith indicates that the cross teaches us by destroying our pride, making us rely on God alone, teaching us patience and obedience.[5] The hard things, like an illness or job loss, have the capacity to teach us how to live before God. Such calamities show us how frail our lives are and how dependent we are upon God. Calvin suggests that "we are by nature too inclined to attribute everything to our own flesh."[6]

An illness can make us realize how vulnerable is our body. How quickly the threat of death makes us realize our dependence upon God. And in turning to God in our weakness and finitude we are strengthened by God's power.

In times of tribulation, God teaches us about the divine faithfulness. Nothing comes to us without God's being with us. As the cross reminds us of God's presence, it immediately connects us with the sustaining power of God's faithfulness.

In the letter to Corinth, the apostle prays, "Blessed be the God and Father of our Lord Jesus Christ, the Father of mercies and the God of all consolation, who consoles us in all our affliction, so that we may be able to console those who are in any affliction with the consolation with which we ourselves are consoled by God" (2 Cor. 1:3-4). In affliction the people of God may count on the constancy of divine mercy. Calvin adds, "The saints . . . experience the fact that God . . . provides the assistance that he has promised."[7]

The cross also teaches us patience. Under the stress of affliction, we search eagerly for release. Nothing pleases us so much as a place to lay down our cross. Yet the purpose of the cross is to teach us to look patiently to the Lord, to wait until the lesson has been fully learned.

The cross teaches obedience. Patience suggests persistence in a long obedience. Bearing the cross keeps us on the path of doing what God has commanded. Perhaps these fruits led our mentor to say that the cross is to "test their patience and to instruct them in obedience."[8] Is it not recorded that even Christ learned obedience through the things which he suffered? (See Hebrews 5:8.)

Second, the cross can be an occasion for chastisement, that is, disciplined correction. Adversity should not take us by surprise. The Lord corrects all those who are members of the family. "My child, do not despise the LORD's discipline or be weary of his reproof, for the LORD reproves the one he loves, as a father the son in whom he delights" (Prov. 3:11-12).

If the cross has been given for our discipline, it originates in God's loving hands. All persons require this discipline to make their lives pure and singular in dedication. The writer of Hebrews states: "If you do not have that discipline in which all children share, then you are illegitimate and not his children" (Heb. 12:8).

Recognizing both the reality and importance of chastisement, when the cross falls upon us we ought to examine our lives. An examination helps us determine whether the cross represents a source of new learning or should be seen as an instrument of instruction or a rod of discipline. Calvin instructs us that "whenever we are afflicted, remembrance of our past life ought immediately to come to mind; so we shall doubtless find that we have committed something deserving this sort of chastisement."[9] Chastened by the Lord, we must be quick to turn to God in repentance and acceptance of the deserved discipline.

Finally, the reason for the cross in our lives may be persecution. For Calvin this cross meant the "defense of the gospel" plus being persecuted in a just cause. Persecution is but one of the means God uses to prepare us for fellowship with our Lord.[10] In a land of religious freedom, we rarely think about suffering persecution for the sake of the gospel. Yet even in a free land, the defense of the gospel and the promotion of righteousness can meet with stiff opposition.

Take, for example, a young man who had climbed the ladder of success to near the top in a multinational corporation. Disillusioned with the "American success syndrome," he had an open heart for the gospel. In the providence of God, a preacher of the truth with a passion for social righteousness entered his life. The corporate executive was converted.

After living in an alternative Christian community for a few years, the evil of war and the destructive power of nuclear arms obsessed this maturing Christian. He felt called to protest in every way he could. As a consequence of his choice and his courageously laying down his life for the gospel, he has spent at least half of his Christian life in jail charged with civil disobedience. When someone points out the slight odds of his actions making a difference in foreign policy or military activity, he responds, "If the unthinkable catastrophe should come, I know that at least I tried." As we feel the pain of this brother's sufferings, we are reminded that Barth emphasized that "those who know what the cross is will not desire or seek to bear it. Self-sought suffering has nothing whatever to do with participation in the passion of Jesus Christ."[11]

Perhaps the defense of the gospel and the promotion of social righteousness will create crosses for us. When we chal-

lenge the stranglehold of the dominant culture on our lives
and the cause and effect elements that compose it, we may
expect persecution. Questioning American foreign policy
earns one the label of unpatriotic or, worse, "Communist."
Providing sanctuary for refugees or withholding taxes used to
finance defense draws the accusation of treason; talking
about a New Creation in which the powerless are energized,
the marginalized included in decision making, and the poor
given the necessities for survival draws disparaging charges
of idealism or sheer fantasy.

Does anyone relish the rejection given a faithful witness to
the gospel? From other perspectives, those who protest the
death penalty meet the same hostility; persons who speak out
against homophobia are likely to be branded "one of them";
those who protest the destruction of the environment often
meet similar persecutions. Christians do face persecution for
their defense of the gospel and their efforts to change the
social structure to provide the benefits of equality and inclu-
siveness to all. Is it possible that only the silent and the
detached escape the cross of persecution?

Beyond the Cross—Truth

Crosses do fall upon all of us. Only the very young and the
cowardly have failed to feel the weight of the cross. In due
time, the cross comes to all unless we compromise our faith.
How we respond makes the difference in the effect of the
cross. John H. Leith says, "A burden becomes a cross only
when we willingly accept it and use it in the light of God's
revelation of his will in the scripture and in experience."[12]
Only those who acknowledge the cross, and accept it as an
instrument of God, grow from their experience.

We suspect that most of us pass through different stages in
our embrace of our particular crosses. When the sight of the
cross first appears before our eyes, the shock may be too great
for us to grasp its meaning. Denial often follows shock in an
effort to avoid the cross. Denials buttressed by fear and anger
can persist for a long time. Only when we slice our way
through all these resistances can we finally embrace the cross
and accept it as the instrument of God. Not until our eyes
have been opened by acceptance can we begin to discern the
purposes of God. Sharing the cross with Christ also helps
take away our bitterness.

Surely beyond our acceptance and the fulfillment of God's purposes of instruction, discipline, and maturity, there must be a place of celebration, a degree of fulfillment with subjective dimensions of joy. The writer of Hebrews says that Jesus "for the sake of the joy that was set before him endured the cross, disregarding its shame, and has taken his seat at the right hand of the throne of God" (Heb. 12:2). Calvin sometimes felt that to treat ourselves softly and with indulgence would make us like "mettlesome horses," for if "fattened in idleness for some days, they cannot afterward be tamed for their high spirits; nor do they recognize their rider, whose command they previously obeyed."[13] Yet we need not become mettlesome horses to rejoice in new insights, deeper maturity, and a quiet patience.

Calvin knew well that beyond the cross stood the empty tomb—resurrection.[14] If the cross means the destruction of the flesh and all that opposes God, the resurrection speaks of new life, wholeness, and freedom to become what God intended. Paul states, "For if we have been united with him in a death like his, we will certainly be united with him in a resurrection like his" (Rom. 6:5). Participation in his resurrection enables us to live in newness of life. We not only die to sin, but we come "alive to God in Jesus Christ" (Rom. 6:11). What kind of aliveness flows from our participation in his resurrection?

Beyond the cross we participate in a new depth of self-awareness. The cross always reveals the depth of our propensity for evil and its constant allurement for us. But this awful awareness of self has turned us toward God. The deeper our awareness of human frailty, the stronger and more deeply do we attach ourselves to God.

Beyond the cross our disciplined and chastened spirits enter more deeply into fellowship with God. The purging action of the cross causes us to desire God and prepares us to be receptive to God's will for our lives. Not only do we hunger for God, but our perceptions are sharpened to recognize God's action in all aspects of our lives.

Beyond the cross, we experience freedom. Sin always has a blinding, enslaving effect on our lives. As the cross frees us from our sinfulness, we have greater freedom to obey God.

As our Lord did, beyond the cross we too experience joy. Our joy rises from the grace and mercy shown to us; it feeds on the transformation that suffering works in our hearts; it is the gift of a gracious God who permits us to sit with Christ in heavenly triumph over sin and death!

In every aspect of the cross, one element of Reformed spirituality shines through: our spirituality consists of the flesh-and-blood reality of our daily lives. God comes to us in everything that happens to us. The joy, sorrow, and routine of our lives constitute the substance with which our faith must deal.

Self-denial and carrying the cross, whether it be instruction, chastisement, or the result of persecution, intends always to bring us into a deepened relationship with God. One medium of divine revelation consists of the difficult circumstances of our everyday lives—the crosses we are asked to bear.

Questions for Reflection

1. What is the meaning of cross bearing?
2. What purposes of the cross does Calvin name?
3. What is the difference between a cross and a calamitous event?
4. Do you honestly believe that hard things in life speak to us of God's purpose for us? Why?
5. How can the church, as a Christian community, help persons bear their crosses?

9

Meditation
on the
Future Life

After two and a half years, Mary and Peter had become settled in the life of First Church in Middletown. Mary's awakened interest in religion had resulted in dramatic changes in her worldview and lifestyle. One Sunday morning she stayed home from church nursing a cold. Since her own church's service of worship was not broadcast, she turned on the television and watched two half-hour church services back-to-back.

During the first program, the minister assured her that the gospel was for here and now, not some pie-in-the-sky payoff for being good. He said, "God wants the best for his children—health, happiness, and prosperity. If you lack these necessities, all you need do is call upon God, and they will be given you, if you but believe!"

This emphasis seemed somewhat different from Dr. Makemie's. She had stressed the importance of accepting the crosses which come to us, of finding them a means of grace. Yet here was a minister of the gospel preaching "health and wealth" as a reward for heroic believing. It seemed a little superficial to Mary.

Immediately following the first minister, another spoke who sounded very much like the minister in her childhood church. He said, "Love not the world, neither the things that are in the world. No matter what loss you may suffer in this life, heaven will be worth it all!" He made it clear that nothing mattered but faith in Jesus Christ as one's Lord and Savior.

"What a contrast," Mary thought to herself. "I wonder where the truth lies. Is faith in Christ for a better life, or is it to be sure of heaven when we die; or is there some other way of orienting myself to life as a faithful disciple of Jesus Christ?" Off and on throughout the following week, Mary pondered the fragile, tenuous, ambiguous nature of her life and the almost overwhelming thought of eternity and eternal life. How were the two related and what did this have to do with the way she lived before God?

Can you imagine the surprise and delight she experienced when she received the church's newsletter and saw Sunday's sermon topic—"All This and Heaven Too!" Text: Colossians 3:2–3: "Set your minds on things that are above, not on things that are on earth, for you have died, and your life is hidden with Christ in God." A brief word of explanation followed—"Helps for evaluating life's experiences in the light of eternity."

In living the Christian life, Calvin emphasized three acts— self-denial, cross bearing, and meditation on the future life. Each of these activities involves the Christian in the context of his or her life. Clearly, each relates to our experience of God. The last of the three, meditation on the future life, thrusts us into the complex issue raised by the televangelists and Dr. Makemie's sermon: How are we to evaluate daily experience in light of eternity, that is, in light of God's will? What must be our attitude toward the world? What use should be made of our hope of heaven? And all these questions converge in the larger issue of the lifestyle called forth by the Reformed faith.

Calvin gives adequate evidence to identify the second TV preacher with himself; at times he discounts the world and emphasizes the vanity of life. In his writings Calvin seems ever conscious of the attraction of the world, the illusion of human immortality, the alien nature of our earthly pilgrimage, and the fear of death that obsesses so many. To combat these obstacles to spiritual growth, Calvin recommends meditation on the future life.

Calvin astutely observed the course of human life and rightly discerned the powerful attraction of the world. When humans reject God as the center of their worship, they instinctively turn to the things of this world to satisfy their hungers. Calvin says that if you examine the plans, the efforts, the deeds of most persons, you will find nothing else but earth. He offers a graphic description of persons allured by earthly values. "Now our blockishness arises from the fact that our minds, stunned by the empty dazzlement of riches, power, and honors, become so deadened that they can see no farther." Not only does the earth deaden the mind, it also seduces the heart. "The heart also, occupied with avarice, ambition, and lust, is so weighed down that it cannot rise up higher."[1] Is it not true that earth still holds a profound attraction for persons—even Christians? Let Christians consider the fulfillment of the future life and live modest, simple, disciplined lives on this earth.

Coupled with this temptation of absorption in the world, Calvin observed that persons live with the illusion of immortality. In their deception, persons cease to recognize that life passes away like smoke (Ps. 102:3) and that their days are no more than an evening shadow (Ps. 102:11). In such a situation it behooves no one to live as if death will never come. Contemplation of the future would surely cure this illusion.

Calvin also recognized the enslavement caused by the widespread fear of death. He deplored the fact "that many who boast themselves Christians are gripped by such a great fear of death. . . . "[2] How can a Christian fear death when it is a promise of release, redemption of the body, more fully clothed with immortality? One ought rather to look forward to the life to come. (See 2 Cor. 5:2–3.)

Furthermore, Calvin insisted that by comparison, the future life made the present seem as nothing. To describe the attitude toward our present life, he used words like "hatred," "contempt," "despised," "loathed," and "miserable condition." This present life compares to a sepulcher from which we are to be raised; it is an alien country in which we are pilgrims passing through on our way to the homeland. Since we are pilgrims, our attachment ought to be more to the homeland than to this alien country.

What Calvin has said about the transient nature of life, its vile, corrupting effect upon Christians, plus his evaluation of life as miserable and a grave from which to be raised, has led many to judge him as denying the world. Granted, his language shows contempt for the world, but this does not discount the value of life on earth; rather, it clarifies the Christian's perspective on the use of and enjoyment of life's pleasures. Calvin's insistence upon meditation on the future life is an effort, not to escape responsibility for the present, but to keep in focus the Christian's goal and to nourish the Christian's hope. All denial of self and earth's allurements are for something better, the enjoyment of life with God and service to our neighbor. Calvin certainly demonstrated in his own life and ministry a healthy concern for this world.

Why does Calvin employ these strong negations of earthly life, and why does he urge us to meditate on the future life? We believe Calvin jealously guarded the intention of God to be in fellowship with the elect community of faith. God desires to be supreme in our lives, as the first commandment tells us. God intends that our chief end be to bring glory to God, as the first question of the Westminster Shorter Catechism makes clear. If we give ourselves to meditation on the future life, our love for and devotion to God will deepen.

This clear focus on our supreme purpose saves us from idolatry. The deep hungers of the human heart when denied their rightful focus on God fix themselves upon substitutes. In biblical language, this misplaced love is idolatry. Idolatry is "the love of the creation instead of the creator." By meditation on the future life, Calvin intends to help us break the grip of worldly substitutes for God.

And we believe Calvin admonishes us to meditate on the future life to inspire our courage and to strengthen our perseverance. Life does have its pain and sufferings; it thrusts crosses upon every shoulder; and if this life were all there is, how could we have hope for the future? The Christian life, which is one of fellowship with God, must be lived amid the attractions of earth without becoming attached to them, and Christians must find courage to persist when temptations seek to turn them from the pathway.

Communion with the Risen Christ

Ronald S. Wallace gives a clearer, more personal, focus on Calvin's call for meditation on the future life. He suggests that in the larger context of Calvin's thought, he is calling for a focus on Christ. To meditate on Christ is to meditate on the future; he has not only been raised from death, he has ascended. Thus, by meditation on the future life Calvin means "that we commune with the risen Christ, and the focal point of such *meditatio* is the ascended Christ."[3]

If we have died with Christ, been raised with him, hidden in God with him, the focus of our life cannot be in this world, but will be in that which is yet to come. This identification with Christ means a reorientation of life—life lived for the future, and thus life in hope.

Wallace emphasizes this point: "The Christian life is a life that strains toward a completion and fulfillment that belongs to it only beyond death. It finds the present full of meaning and purpose only because it knows that the future has meaning and certainty. It is a constant and bold march through the darkness of this world to the day of resurrection."[4] Because of the resurrection and the ascension of Christ, our lives have a future orientation. The future has security and promise because of him, and we live in hope because of his promise.

Though the fulfillment of our lives awaits the future, we do experience the new life of Christ in the present. But we must "regard the gift of 'life' which we now increasingly enjoy in Christ as but a pledge of ultimate 'fullness of life.' "[5] So the present offers a taste of the fulfillment that awaits us, and because we have the first roots of this new life in the present, we can imagine the fulfillment it will bring in the future. This present fulfillment suggests a partial realization, a foretaste of what the future holds in plentitude.

The Christian life is lived in the world; it is not a world-denying style of life. The Fourth Gospel presents further evidence in support of the notion that the Christian life is not world-denying. John Leith defends the Reformed view by stating, "There is a firm basis in Calvin's writing for interpreting meditation on the future life in the Johannine sense of present participation in eternal life here on earth."[6] In the Gospel of John, eternal life is both a present possession and a future realization.

The first mention of life in John's Gospel can be found in his brilliant prologue. "What has come into being in him was life" (John 1:3–4). The word (*logos*), which was from the beginning with God, was God, and through him all creation came into being; in him was life. And the life which came into being through him was "the light of all people." The life that is in him he willingly shares with all.

We participate in this eternal life in Christ by believing in him. As Moses lifted up the serpent in the wilderness, so Jesus, the Representative Man, was lifted up "that whoever believes in him may have eternal life" (John 3:15). This lifting up of the son of God reveals God's great love for us (John 3:16).

Christ can give us this life because he has life within himself, just as God does. He is not a contingent being like us, but has within himself the life-power, and he "gives life to whomever he wishes" (John 5:21).

John compares this life to bread. Perhaps these insights arose the day Jesus fed the multitude, or maybe later as a part of a Communion ritual. Whatever stimulated the insights, John sees Jesus as "the bread of life" (John 6:35), as the bread "which comes down from heaven and gives life to the world" (John 6:33). This Johannine view begins not with the ascension, but with the incarnation. He who was the essence of life entered into the world in order to share life with those destined to die.

Yet the life he gives to the world is not merely the preservation of life in the face of death, but a new quality of life—eternal life, life with a lasting, fulfilling quality. Jesus testified to this when he said, "I came that they may have life, and have it abundantly" (John 10:10). Jesus makes the same point of fullness of life by saying, "My flesh is true food and my blood is true drink" (John 6:55).

Jesus also contrasts the eternal life, which he gives, with the life the world offers. "Those who love their life lose it, and those who hate their life in this world will keep it for eternal life" (John 12:25). To love one's own life means to value oneself above all else, to do with life what one pleases without regard for the will of God. To hate one's life means that by comparison to our love for Christ and his will for us, our self-regard appears as hatred. This attitude does not suggest a negative rejection of the self, but a rejection of all life separated from God. Once again this contrast emphasizes the distinction between fulfilling human appetites and doing the will of God.

This eternal life, for which we have been created and from which we have been separated, comes to us through Christ. He is the way to God, the truth about God, and the embodiment of the life of God (John 14:6). The manner of our lives, the understanding we have of life, and the energy to live through tests and tribulations, come from Christ who has given and continues to give us eternal life.

In the end, Jesus states the meaning of eternal life as the knowledge of God and knowledge of himself. "And this is eternal life, that they may know you, the only true God, and Jesus Christ whom you have sent" (John 17:3). Does this not summarize the Johannine understanding of eternal life? The word in whom life existed came into the world to share it with all people; those who believe in him will see life, and those who partake of his flesh and blood nourish this life; this life is abundant and fulfilling and makes a pure earthly life appear as refuge; and this existence revealed in Christ as the way, the truth, and the life comes to fulfillment in the knowledge of God. Meditation on eternal life, which we now have in Christ, therefore enables us to discern properly our earthly values and attachments.

This brief excursion into John's Gospel supports Leith's notion that meditation on the future life can be understood as a contemplation of Christ who gives to us life here and now and fulfills this life in eternity. Sharing in the resurrection/ ascension of Christ and the present participation in eternal life undergirds a positive evaluation of the present life. The common life has value because it is life mediated through Christ. Receptivity and appreciation of this life strengthens its power in us. Meditation on the future gives focus for the present and the hope of fulfillment for what is now preliminary and anticipatory.

Meditation on the future life has an intent similar to self-denial and cross bearing. Calvin calls us to deny ourselves in order that we may give ourselves to God in complete devotion; he tells us to bear the cross so that we may have a relationship with God through our trials and tribulations; and he urges us to meditate on the future life so that we may properly value, orient, and fulfill the present one.

A Call to Christian Meditation

In view of the emphasis on meditation on the future life, how does a contemporary person of faith engage in this perspective on life? To describe Calvin's approach to meditation, Wallace uses phrases like: "intensity of aim," "concentration of the whole mind," "true and holy thinking," "deep desire for the life of heaven," and "with the whole heart."[7] These phrases suggest that meditation engages the mind and heart in a deep desire for God. In contrast with the mystics, Calvin did not engage in mind-emptying meditation but in filling the mind with "true and holy" thoughts, especially words of scripture. He found it most helpful to meditate on "holy history"; and he liked to use the words of the Psalms as his prayers. To engage in this type of serious reflection upon God required a certain amount of discipline to clear and to focus the mind.

While there are numerous ways to approach growth in this discipline, perhaps one helpful approach to the contemporary practice of meditation would be to clear the mind of competing loyalties so that we may focus on Christ and eternal life. The initial step in meditation should be self-examination. In what ways are we absorbed in the life of the world? Are our goals in life shaped by *Playboy, The Wall Street Journal,* and the American model of success, or by the life of simplicity and service exemplified in Jesus Christ? Consider our consumerism and greed. We live in a world of leveraged buyouts, corporate presidents with salaries of $450,000 a month, and athletes getting $5,000,000 per year. Do we not need to modify the excessive hold the world has upon us? We must not despise the blessings of life, sinking into a gloomy austerity, nor can we let ourselves buy everything we desire. A contemplation of the future will lead to moderation, frugality, and sobriety. We must live as stewards who have been given a trust from the owner of all.

In what way are we different from the rich young man who asked Jesus the way to eternal life? We suspect many of us would experience his sadness if Jesus said to us, "If you wish to be perfect, go, sell your possessions, and give the money to the poor . . . then come, follow me" (Matt. 19:21).

Does not the illusion that we are immortal also distract us from meditation? Our inordinate fear of death entices us to buy into this illusion. The fear of death is one of the greatest fears in our culture today. In how many ways do we hide from our own death? We secure the future with savings and insurance; we support research in transplants so that when body parts wear out, we may use another's; we disguise death with beautiful flowers, expensive caskets, and cosmetic appearances so that persons say, "She looks as natural as in life." If these actions do not ward off the fear of death, we fill our minds with plans, deals, new wishes—anything to block out the thought of our mortality. How can we meditate on God when our minds are filled with earthly things?

Meditation on the future life gives a different perspective on the present life. When we consider that our home is with God, the ultimate fulfillment of our lives is God, and that the life we have on earth is perishing—these contrasts help us to evaluate life properly. The man who tore down his barns to build larger ones lacked this perspective. (See Luke 12:18.) Like many of us, he was living with a false set of values based on the illusion that his life would continue as it always had. We suspect meditation on eternal life will suffer until we release our grip on matters temporal.

If we can face the painful assessment of our values, as Wallace suggests, our minds can be freed to focus on Christ. Meditation on Christ should include his person, his promises, and his passion. Consider first his person. Our knowledge of Christ comes from the Gospels, especially the Synoptics. We have found great benefit in reading about and contemplating the encounter of Jesus with the paralytic, for example (Mark 2:1–12). After reading this story, close your eyes and picture the sequence of events. With these aspects of the narrative in mind, identify with the paralyzed man. What did he feel? What thoughts came to his mind? What decisions did he make? How did he feel about Jesus? These reflections let you become part of the story. When you have become identified with the paralyzed man, think of the questions which come naturally to your mind. Ask Jesus these questions. After each question, listen in your heart for his reply. Writing down your thoughts will help you express yourself and remember your impressions.

Meditate on the promises of Christ. A meditation on the Sermon on the Mount focuses our attention on the basic content of Jesus' teaching (Matt. 5–7). Suppose you begin with the beatitudes—"Blessed are the poor in spirit, for theirs is the kingdom of heaven" (Matt. 5:3). Hold each word in your mind, associate freely with it. Connect one phrase to the other, let the whole verse grasp you. Ask questions: Who are the poor in spirit? What does "blessed" mean? What is the kingdom of heaven? What does it mean to possess it? After this disciplined reflection, try being quiet before the text. Instead of working on the text, let the text work on you.

Calvin found meditation on Christ's passion most beneficial. Use the suggestions we have already made, and apply them to accounts of Jesus' arrest, trial, and crucifixion (Matt. 26:47–27:66; Mark 14:43–15:47; Luke 22:47–23:56). As you read, reflect, envision, and experience his passion, let the reality of God's great love draw you into Christ's suffering.

If we can clear our minds from absorption in the desires of earth and meditate on Christ's person, promises, and passion, we can be freed to live the Christ life, eternal life. In our brief examination of eternal life in the Gospel of John, we discovered that it represents a quality of life. The writer of this fourth Gospel calls it eternal life, and he means the life of the future experienced in the present. The very life of God which was in Christ has been given to us as a foretaste of eternity, and we experience it now in our daily encounters.

Meditation on the future life surely includes a reflection on the forgiveness of sin. Through Christ, we know today the forgiveness of all our sins. Imagine a conscience freed from guilt, no basis in us for self-condemnation, no inhibitions generated by the neurotic fear of judgment and punishment.

In the present, we meditate on the knowledge of God. Christ has made God known to us. Our meditation deepens our awareness of the divine love, guidance, and protection. All things in our lives pass through the hands of a loving God.

This new life in Christ is fellowship with God (1 John 1:1-3). We have a relationship with God. Think about it! We mortals have fellowship with the eternal God. Through Christ our earthly lives have been reoriented by a magnetic attraction to the Center Point of the universe.

Through the eternal life given us in Christ, we have fulfillment—the satiation of our deepest desires. We long to be, to survive, and Christ promises us the conquest of death. "I am the resurrection and the life" (John 11:25). Our hearts long for security in the face of threats. Only Christ can be with us when we walk through "the valley of the shadow of death." He meets our deep longings for community, the desire to belong to a significant person and to a loving group. He has promised to accept us if we come to him; in his body, the church, we find genuine acceptance when we come into it. In him we also find our sense of worth. We feel worth not because of our status, but because we have been stamped in his image and redeemed by his death. All of these fulfillments belong to us because of the eternal life bestowed upon us by Christ.

The eternal life bestowed upon us carries with it meaning. Meaning must surely be the knowledge of God, the fellowship with God, and the fulfillment of our earthly lives. Meaning begins in the concreteness of our broken, empty lives. The meaning of our lives gives to us a sense of purpose; it provides direction. And the glorious promise of Christ guarantees that death cannot snuff out the meaning of the unique persons God created us to become.

Are not these facets of eternal life worthy of our meditation and expressions of spontaneous gratitude? If we but let our minds focus on this gracious gift of Christ, will not the recollection of his benefits stir us to action? Meditation on the future life will also make us more determined to free ourselves of earthly idols and to give our attention to those pursuits God desires for us.

What a glorious life Christ has given us! Yet the fullness of eternal life will always be hampered throughout our mortal life by the limitation of our physical body. Our bodies have been corrupted by sin and are destined to die. Perhaps our meditation on eternal life begins a transition toward the promise of the new body: "For this perishable body must put on imperishability, and this mortal body must put on immortality" (1 Cor. 15:53).

When our mortality has slipped on the coat of immortality, all that has been forecast by our preliminary tastes of eternal life will then be brought to fulfillment (2 Cor. 5:1–5; 1 Cor. 15:54–56). In that day when we experience the fullness of eternal life, not a mere foretaste, we will know not only forgiveness of sin but also freedom from sin. Our incomplete knowledge of God will be expanded, and we shall "know fully, even as [we] have been fully known" (1 Cor. 13:12). The fellowship with God, which has been veiled, will then be face to face (1 Cor. 13:12). The fragmentary fulfillment that we now experience will be complete when we are "filled with all the fullness of God" (Eph. 3:19). In this eternal life, all the meaning in our lives and all the meaning created throughout history shall be judged and refined and retained in the eternal memory of God. And the God who created the world and shared life with us creatures will grant to us an eternity with God—three in one, Father, Son, and Holy Spirit. This excursion into meditation may explain why Calvin says, "No one has made progress in the school of Christ who does not joyfully await the day of death and final resurrection."[8]

Let no one say this is too much "pie in the sky by and by." Either eternal life is true, or it is not. If it is true, meditation on its various aspects reorients earth to heaven.

Questions for Reflection

1. Is meditation on the future life an escape from earthly responsibility? Give reasons for your answer.
2. What does the Gospel of John mean by eternal life? How does this perspective illuminate the meaning of Calvin's use of the term "future life"?
3. What present value is there in meditation on the future life?
4. What causes human beings to resist meditation on the future life?
5. What effect would this discipline have on the life of a congregation?

RESPONSIBILITIES OF THE CHRISTIAN LIFE

10

Spirituality
as Love
for Neighbor

Three years had passed since that April morning when
Peter and Mary joined the First Presbyterian Church. One
cool autumn afternoon after they returned from church, the
phone rang and Mary answered. It was Bill Carrier, moderator of the nominating committee at First Church. He set up
an appointment with Mary for later in the afternoon.

"I wonder what that's all about," Mary said, when she
hung up the phone. "Bill Carrier from the nominating committee wants to come by and talk with me."

"If he spoke about the nominating committee," replied
Peter, "he probably wants to ask you to be an officer. We are
electing three new elders and three new deacons next month."

Peter's hunch proved correct. "Mary," Bill said, "the entire
committee felt that you have demonstrated the qualities required for a deacon. You care for people, you have worked in
the shelter for homeless women, you have visited shut-ins.
Since deacons have a responsibility to minister to persons in
need, we thought you would be an excellent choice."

Affirmed and stunned, Mary said, "Can you tell me a little
more about the office of deacon?"

Bill explained that the diaconate originated in the early
church when a group of widows complained that they were
being neglected in the distribution of food. The apostles
called the disciples together to choose seven persons to han-
dle the charitable relief work—this action set the apostles
free to preach. The seven men chosen were not called deacons,
but they were like the later deacons mentioned in the New
Testament. "Dr. Makemie will answer your questions in the

officers' training class," Bill promised. "We hope you will
think and pray about accepting this call. I'll get back to you in
a few days for your decision."

When Bill left, Mary talked over her decision with Peter.
At first, she didn't know what to do. Why serve officially as a
deacon when she was already doing many of the things deacons do? And what about all the meetings she would have to
attend—was it worth it? But the more she thought and
prayed about it, the more she sensed the call of God. The
nominating committee had affirmed her gifts for ministry.
She also saw the responsibility as an opportunity to involve
other members in the church's ministry. When Bill called
back, she agreed to serve. The committee placed her name in
nomination before the congregation, and the congregation
elected Mary and two others as deacons.

In her preparation, one thing became clear to Mary about
the ministry of a deacon: Reformed Christians minister to
those in need—the friendless, the sick, the poor, and the
distressed. On the day of ordination, with great excitement,
she stood with her fellow officers before the congregation as
the minister asked, "Will you be a faithful deacon, teaching
charity, urging concern, and directing the people's help to the
friendless and those in need? In your ministry will you try to
show the love and justice of Jesus Christ?"

In a strong, clear voice Mary answered, "I will." She knelt
with the others and was ordained with prayer and laying on of
hands.

The Diaconal Function

Who has been called to show the love of God to the poor and
suffering?

The pastor? Yes.

Elders? Yes.

Deacons? Yes.

Every member of the body of Christ? Yes!

The faith that we profess leads us to show the love of God
to all persons.

Love for God is the first and indispensable part of Calvin's
teaching, but he insisted that we must express our love for
God by loving people. Only by loving people can we prove the
love we profess toward God. Both the law and Jesus himself
state that we are to love our neighbor as ourselves. "Calvin

repeatedly asserts," says John Leith, "that a person's obedience to the second table of the law is the true test of religion."[1] If we truly love God, we will love our neighbor.

If we are all to love our neighbor, why the special emphasis on the deacon? The deacon in the Reformed tradition has the formal responsibility for guiding the church's ministry of compassion in matters like distributing food and caring for the homeless. Since meeting the needs of persons exceeds the ability of a single individual, a corporate response is required from the congregation. Thus the diaconate. The diaconate provides a model of Christian compassion for every follower of Christ.

We have chosen the office of deacon to symbolize the ministry of compassion because it has both a strong biblical foundation and deep roots in the Reformed tradition. From the earliest days in Geneva, the Reformed Church showed compassion to the sick and displaced. To direct this ministry, Calvin reconstituted the office of deacon in sixteenth-century Geneva. The Reformed Church had two classes of deacons: the first class took care of the poor and the sick; the second administered the affairs of the poor. For example, one kind of deacon ran the hospital and the other dealt with the patients. These two roles illustrate the personal and corporate aspects of a ministry of compassion.

When Protestant refugees from Roman Catholic France poured into the city, many had no place to live; others needed clothes; most needed jobs; some were sick; still others were orphans. So the Geneva church created the French Fund for Poor Foreigners (*Bourse Française*). Three deacons were elected to administer this fund. But deacons were more than administrators. Calvin urged the deacons to visit the poor and the sick, a duty written into later ordinances of the French Fund.[2]

As we look back upon the French Fund from the perspective of twentieth-century America, it had an amazing scope and thoroughness. Consider what it achieved: the deacons visited the sick and poor whom they helped; they established orphanages, arranged foster homes for children, provided lodging for overnight visitors and permanent housing for refugees. The deacons made an effort to know the poor to avoid being duped. They provided job training for unemployed persons and hospital care for the sick. The deacons sent Bibles and Psalters into

France, although it was dangerous to do so. What started as a welfare fund ended up as an international fund.

Do we not see how the New Testament office of the deacon was embraced and expanded by Calvin to guide the church's ministry of compassion? This ministry expressed corporately the love of neighbor to which all have been called. Reference to the Geneva church and the French Fund further indicates that the ministry of compassion has roots that reach back to the beginning of our tradition.

But we must ask yet another question: What has the show of compassion to do with Reformed spirituality? For some this question may be superfluous, but for others it will call forth an important notion. For many sincere persons, the word "spirituality" evokes only pictures of prayer, worship, and meditation as devotion to God. But according to Calvin, there can be no true love of God apart from love for our neighbor. While we assuredly experience the love of God in worship and private devotion, we also experience this love in works of compassion. Reformed spirituality, therefore, consists of being and doing. God touches our lives through prayer and compels us to express that love through deeds of mercy.

Can we now envision how the office of deacon offers us a model not only of corporate compassion but also of individuals loving their neighbors? In some sense the whole church is a diaconate of compassion. And the true nature of Reformed spirituality finds expression in both the corporate and the personal aspects of neighbor love. With this conjoining of spirituality and compassion, we must inquire more deeply into the love of our neighbor.

Love for God—Love for Neighbor

Love for God is the foundation from which all our social concern flows. Calvin wrote:

> Since every man is devoted to himself, there will never be true charity toward neighbors unless where the love of God reigns; for it is a mercenary love which the children of the world entertain for each other because every one of them has regard to his own advantage. On the other hand, it is impossible for the love of God to reign without producing brotherly kindness among men.[3]

Thus for Calvin the ability to love our neighbor depends upon a prior love for God. Without this love we are left with a self-centeredness which prohibits love of neighbor. But there can be no love of God that does not include love of neighbor.

But who is our neighbor? In the parable of the Good Samaritan, Jesus taught that our love should go out to all indiscriminately. Such indiscriminate love reflects the "order of nature" by which we are to live, each person bound to every other person. For one to have needs means all have needs; for one to suffer means all suffer. To love God means to love our neighbor, and our neighbor is anyone in need. Spirituality consists of expressing the love of God to those in need.

Self-Denial and Love

But how are we to love our neighbor? We have already observed that Calvin connected self-denial and love for neighbor. To love others we must deny ourselves. Calvin said: "Unless you give up all thought of self and, so to speak, get out of yourself, you will accomplish nothing here."[4] Self cannot be the center of our focus if we are to love others. Yet nothing rubs against our nature more than the subjection of ourselves to the claims of others. One of the best ways to practice such inward self-denial is to force ourselves to perform the duties of charity. The gracious expression of love calls for radical self-denial.

In *Burma Diary* Paul Geren tells about patients being moved from one hospital building to another. Many of the patients had dysentery; the stink was terrible. Geren and a couple of others, one British and one American, watched the Burmese "sweepers" move the patients. They moved slowly; the job had to be done, and no one wanted to do it.

The American turned to the British soldier and said, "I am very glad at this moment that I am agnostic." His denial of faith gave him a reason for leaving the offensive task to the "sweepers."

His British friend did believe and therefore was not free to stand by and watch. Neither was Geren, who said, "Get down in it! Pick the patients up! Soil yourself with this disease! There is no need to call this filthiness sweet, or to start enjoying it through some strange inversion. Only one thing is necessary; for love's sake it must be done."[5]

Geren and his British friend literally forced themselves to move the dysentery victims because for love's sake "it had to be done." Self-denial meant they had to put down all thoughts of revulsion or what they naturally wanted to do. By the grace of God we, too, must examine our lives and deal decisively with all the natural faults and tendencies that keep us from serving the neighbor. This means more than simply being displeased with ourselves; it means saying no to self. The negative side to self-denial means the death of self-centeredness; the positive side requires love of our neighbor and commitment to God. The Spirit of God lives and rules in us. If Reformed spirituality unites in unbreakable bonds the love of God with love of neighbor, then self-denial makes room for the love of God. In some sense, therefore, the depth of our spirituality relates to the denial of self and the enlargement of our capacity to love.

The Image of God

Calvin offered yet another reason for the love of neighbor: humans have been created in the image of God. He said that "Scripture helps in the best way when it teaches that we are not to consider that men merit of themselves but to look upon the image of God in all men, to which we owe all honor and love."[6] Since humans are created in God's image, God must feel wounded and outraged in the person of victims of human cruelty and wickedness. Anyone who hurts another human being made in the image of God injures God. Thus, God commands us to love, and this forbids our injuring another human being.

Do we not feel the weight of Calvin's argument? We have been commanded to love our neighbor, which expresses our depth of spirituality. But more, we are to look upon the neighbor, whether in the affluent family next door or a "bum on the street," as existing in the image of God. To hurt, to offend, or even to ignore either the family next door or the street person brings pain to God.

To serve this neighbor is to minister to God. The need of the neighbor, therefore, invites us to fellowship with God. Does not this insight make the point even more emphatically that our spiritual life is mediated through faithful service, as well as through diligent prayer.

A Common Humanity

Calvin also insists on love of neighbor because all share in a common humanity. No matter what divides us, we cannot despise our own flesh. Humankind issued from a common human parentage, forming one body. Because we share a common humanity, "we cannot but behold, as in a mirror, our own face in those who are poor and despised, who have come to an end of their own power to help themselves, and who groan under their burden, even though they are utter strangers to us."[7]

On the basis of our common humanity, to act with love toward our fellow human beings means that we show ourselves to be human in our relationships with them. This shared humanity directs our relationships in the home, at work, and everywhere else.

What does love of neighbor based on a common humanity imply for Reformed spirituality? To love the neighbor as one who bears the image of God is to honor God. This form of honor to God builds up the human community through the motivation of love. As each member receives the ministry of love, the whole community grows and gathers strength. Thus, to minister to one member of the society who is in need enriches the whole society. Imagine the social problems that would be solved if we showed this kind of neighbor love. Again, we see the tight linkage between the spirituality of love and the life of compassionate service as the hallmark of Reformed spirituality.

Mutual Communication

Still another foundation stone in Calvin's understanding of love of neighbor is "mutual communication." We give to others what they need to enrich the whole of our common life. We have a common habitation in the world, not an infinite number of private worlds. Moreover, we are all part of the one body of Christ. To assist us in mutual communication, God gave us tongues with which to console one another and meet our respective needs. To fail to use God's gift would be to corrupt the order of nature.

Likewise God gave us money as part of the order of nature. To achieve mutual sharing, the rich are to help the poor and offer bread to the hungry. Not to use our money properly means that we corrupt the order of nature. We are not to take pride in sharing our money with the poor, for this is our duty as given by the law of nature. According to this law, each of us must give and each must receive.[8] The rich should not feel self-sufficient; no one is. Each of us needs our neighbor simply to exist. In other words, we live in an interlocking network of human relationships and must share mutual concern for each other.

Reformed spirituality shows compassion for all persons, but the common bond of humanity is not as strong as that which binds us to our fellow Christians in the church. Calvin believed that the image of God shone even more brightly in those who have been regenerated than in other persons, thus creating sacred ties that bind us to our fellow Christians more closely than to those outside the fellowship of the church. "If to injure our fellow man is to pervert the order of nature, to injure our fellow Christian is to 'tear Jesus Christ in pieces.' "[9]

Spirituality as Neighbor Love

Our investigation of the "love of neighbor" makes our engagement with the person in need an unavoidable task for the Christian. Love of God inevitably issues in love of the neighbor, within the church and beyond it. From a practical standpoint, we must ask how baptized persons should show the love of God to others.

We have stressed that our spirituality can never be a private affair, so in our actions of love there must be both a personal and a corporate expression. Nurture, for example, occurs programmatically through worship, church school, and other educational endeavors. But we believe that a nurturing community must be made up of nurturing individuals. How, therefore, can persons express their love of God in the nurturing of fellow members of the church?

Perhaps nurture starts with acquaintance. Take time to know the members of the congregation. This suggestion applies especially to large congregations, or those with rapid turnover in membership. To know means more than facial recognition or the ability to call another's name. How many of us develop a small cluster of friends, greet them in worship, and never bother to expand the radius of our friendship circle?

Persons receive nurture through recognition and affirmation. Special achievements, such as a promotion, a graduation, or the reception of an honor, are opportunities for us to make a phone call, visit, or send a letter in celebration. We nurture others when we acknowledge their accomplishments.

Love means taking persons seriously, and that implies listening to them. In an age characterized by rushing from home to work and back again, listeners are hard to find. Listening sincerely to another's life story, to his or her hopes and dreams and to common interests, is love in action.

Perhaps inclusion offers yet another form of love. Nothing raises questions about our worth any more than being excluded by certain persons or groups. By the same token, nothing offers richer nurture than an invitation to belong to a significant group. A colleague recently experienced this strong inclusion. He was invited to an anniversary celebration. When the places to sit were assigned, he found himself seated with the honorees and their intimate family. Nothing else could have bespoken inclusion so strongly.

Giving gifts, sharing meals and tasks, and lending books could also be considered forms of nurture. Getting acquainted, affirming, listening, and including others adequately illustrates love for our fellow Christians.

Our love for those in the church can also be expressed as pastoral care. Martin Luther had a graphic saying that we are priests to one another. Luther meant that each member has a responsibility to be a priest or pastor to others. If pastoral care of other members expresses our spirituality, how are we to demonstrate it? Each member may help others by being present in the crises of life—birth, illness, catastrophe, and death. These experiences come to all God's people, and the shock and pain are lessened by the presence of a brother or sister in Christ. When fellow Christians are ill or face some other crisis, we go to them. At first we may say nothing; it is enough to be with them.

But love demands more than presence; love requires that we feel with and for those in pain. Inevitably we imagine ourselves in their situation; their distress evokes in us feelings of shock, doubt, and dismay. This empathy provides the context for effective pastoral care shared among the members. At the proper moment, our presence and love will be expressed in words. There are no "correct" words to speak, only words from the heart, which carry the depth of our identification with the suffering of a fellow Christian. In comparison to presence and compassion, words follow at a distance. But words are important; words give expression to the meaning of our presence.

Care also includes doing what is necessary in a particular situation. A friend of ours once expressed this response as "whatever it takes." We are called to give whatever it takes in time, in work, in money, or in personal sacrifice to ease the burden of a brother or sister created in the image of God, a person with whom we share a common humanity and with whom we are called to share mutually.

As Calvin has so clearly pointed out, love of neighbor must not be limited to those within the Christian community. For all the reasons cited, we are to love those who do not believe, who even live in disobedience to God. Even our enemies are subjects of compassion. "Love your enemies," Jesus said, "and pray for those who persecute you, so that you may be children of your Father in heaven; for he makes his sun rise on the evil and on the good, and sends rain on the righteous and on the unrighteous" (Matt. 5:44–45).

How are we to love those persons outside the church? Certainly one way to love is the corporate expression of help through the church. Writing a check may shield us from exposure to the pain of the homeless, the prisoners, the unemployed, and the destitute. Still it aids those who suffer. Deacons must investigate needs and give holistic assistance in ways not possible for every individual.

Yet personal contact with human need in the world will cause us to grow in ways that contributions to the food pantry or a relief fund cannot. Persons outside the church are like those on the inside. They have the same needs, the same dreams and longings, if life has not robbed them of hope. They will benefit, therefore, by the same ministry of presence, compassion, and speech given to those inside the church. They also need material help ministered by our hands. James the apostle once said, "If a brother or sister is naked and lacks daily food, and one of you says to them, 'Go in peace; keep warm and eat your fill,' and yet you do not supply their bodily needs, what is the good of that?" (James 2:15–16).

Would not serving in a soup line, attending a night shelter for the homeless, repairing the homes of the elderly, or building a Habitat for Humanity house show an authentic form of spirituality? If for some reason you cannot, or choose not to, get so close to human need, we challenge you to listen to a beggar on the street. He may stand at a corner with a sign saying, "I am hungry; I will work for food." Or she may approach you in a shopping center with a request for money to buy food for her children. Next time notice these persons. Let yourself "see" them—they bear God's image, they share your humanity, their need demands mutual communication.

When you have taken account of them, ask them about themselves. "Would you tell me, please, what tragic thing has happened which has left you in such need?" Listen to what they say.

And at least one time, without judgment or hesitation, give them money out of your pocket. The next time you may wonder about its use for wine or drugs, but this time give from your abundance with the thought that you are responding to the image of God, to a person who mirrors your own self, were you not the recipient of undeserved mercy.

As no other, we believe the Reformed tradition unites with unbreakable bonds the love of God with the love of neighbor. We purposely have challenged you to authenticate your spirituality by offering nurture and care to fellow Christians and compassion to those who are not yet believers. Not only will your mercy help another, you will receive more than you give!

The sensitive reader will have begun to wonder if we think a little food, a few clothes, and a handout will cure the problems of the poor. No, we are painfully aware that compassion does not penetrate to the root causes of the issues we have raised. In the next chapter we will see how Reformed spirituality leads us to work toward reconciliation, a task which requires us to challenge systems and structures. Or as Paul stated it, we must struggle "against the cosmic powers of this present darkness, against the spiritual forces of evil in the heavenly places" (Eph. 6:12).

Questions for Reflection

1. Who is our neighbor?
2. What does it mean to love the neighbor?
3. How does Calvin distinguish between the neighbor in the church and those outside the church?
4. What forms of neighbor love can be expressed inside the church?
5. How is love of neighbor an expression of spirituality?
6. How effective is your congregation in loving the neighbor?

11

Spirituality
as Reconciliation
in the World

The joint meeting of the officers at First Presbyterian Church erupted in animated discussion. The elders and deacons were together in early December to finalize the budget, which the elders had prepared. Since the budget included a number of items involving the work of the deacons, the session had wisely called the meeting to get the deacons' input. Under the category of benevolences, Mary noticed a reduction in the amount allocated for the homeless shelter from ninety-five hundred dollars to eighty-five hundred dollars.

"Why the one thousand dollar cut in the budget for the homeless shelter?" asked Mary.

Don Holt, moderator of the budget committee, cleared his throat and said: "Frankly, our committee thought that we were spending too much on the shelter, and we decided to cut back. And also First Church's involvement with the shelter has become quite controversial."

"Controversial?" asked Mary. "What do you mean?"

"Well," replied Don, "I didn't want to get into this, but some of our members have been upset because Dr. Makemie appeared before the city council recently and asked the council to appropriate money for public toilets for the homeless. Jack Mason, a member of the council and one of our church members, told us he didn't think ministers should be meddling in the council's affairs. Two months ago, Dr. Makemie also appeared before the council to request that money be appropriated to buy bus tokens for the homeless so that they could get to work each day."

"Good for her!" said Mary. "And next month I'll go with her." Mary was so angry she was clenching her chair.

"Guess it's time for me to respond," said Dr. Makemie, who had been quiet until this point. "I had no idea that my advocacy for the homeless would cause any repercussions. But I see my assumption was false. I must say that it is our responsibility as Christians to get involved in the problems of our society. And we certainly have a problem in this city with homeless people."

"It's a problem of their own choosing!" said Frances Wollenski, a long-time elder. "Listen, if you gave every one of them a new house, they couldn't manage it. They would probably sell it to buy drugs and be back here in our shelter in a month."

"Some may not be able to manage," Mary shot back, "but that's no reason to deny them aid. You've cut a big chunk out of the shelter's budget. We can't operate effectively on an eighty-five-hundred-dollar budget."

The debate went on for more than an hour. At ten o'clock they adjourned after agreeing to meet the following Sunday. Mary lingered for a few minutes after the meeting to support Dr. Makemie and get her direction. Still angry when she left the church that night, Mary went home to tell Peter what had happened.

What an incredible irony that even in our day the controversy over social action continues to surface in church after church. Many in Presbyterian and Reformed churches have forgotten their heritage, have never been instructed in it, or have been influenced by suspect dogma.

The former Presbyterian Church in the United States long held a doctrine of "the spirituality of the church." Dr. Ernest Trice Thompson, well-known historian of the southern church, pointed out that though southern Presbyterians contributed much to the fabric of the new nation during the colonial period, they also developed the doctrine of the spirituality of the church, which silenced the church's social witness.

An influential southern Presbyterian, John Holt Rice, considered slavery a tremendous evil and prayed that the nation might be delivered from it. Rice sensed that sentiment was growing *against* slavery among southern people; he also sensed resentment toward the church and its ministers as they became more involved in this moral issue. Rice feared that further church involvement would actually *hinder* the antislavery movement. Under those conditions, writes Dr. Thompson, he reached the following conclusion: "Let the church confine itself to making good Christians"—that, and that only.[1] Rice took this position to aid the work of abolition and to preserve the unity of the church.

A colleague of Rice's, James Henley Thornwell, became a strong proponent of the spirituality of the church. For Thornwell the questions surrounding slavery were "not for the Church but for the State, not for ministers but statesmen. Christian men may discuss them as citizens and patriots, but not as members of the Church of Jesus Christ." He also said that the church "is not a moral institute of universal good, whose business it is to wage war upon every form of human ill . . . *It has no commission to construct society afresh . . . to change the forms of its political constitutions.*"[2] And this doctrine is by no means dead.

Similar thinking created controversy in the former United Presbyterian Church. The Confession of 1967 was produced amid fierce controversy; it emphasized reconciliation. Conflict arose when the Confession addressed such burning questions as racial discrimination, the arms race, enslaving poverty, and the inequality of women and men. The Confession plainly said: "Our generation stands in peculiar need of reconciliation in Christ."[3] So the conflict at the officers' meeting in Middletown arose from different views of the church. One group wanted the church to deal with "souls" and leave social issues to the government; the other group demanded that the gospel be socially relevant.

Separating souls from social issues and placing the church in a "spiritual" category unrelated to the world produces a gnostic spirituality. This separation falsely splits persons into souls and bodies and divides life into spiritual and material sectors. Such segregation is not biblical. In terms of living the Christian life, the Bible knows nothing of soulless bodies or bodiless souls. The Bible affirms God's love for all creation. God cares about the whole person and about whatever affects humans for good or ill. Believing God is active in all of life, the Reformed tradition encourages us to join God in God's work in the world where we meet God, serve God, and experience abundant life. Worldly witness is part—a vital part—of Reformed spirituality. Does not our social action demonstrate God's redemptive activity in the world? Is such action not a dimension of Reformed spirituality?

The Teachings of Calvin

To determine properly Calvin's teachings in regard to Christian responsibility for society, we must place the individual in society—the two cannot be looked at apart from each other. Consider a great drama taking place: the interaction of God, humans, and the world. Here is the way the drama unfolded.

God created the world. And God created humans in God's image and intended for them to live in a pattern of order. God wanted humans to be witnesses to the beauty and glory of the Creator, living a life of ordered integrity and righteousness. This ordered life included social relationships, best modeled in marriage and the family.

In this intended pattern of order God wanted Adam and Eve to have dominion and lordship over the world. Humans were supposed to possess and enjoy the earth in all of its goodness and fruitfulness, yet not find the true meaning of life in this present order. Rather, God wanted us to meditate on the better and heavenly life to come.[4]

Enter the Fall! Adam and Eve rebelled against God, and their act had disastrous consequences for humankind. Since the Fall we are bereft of a clear and unambiguous trace of the original order of creation. Instead of being witnesses to the beauty and glory of God, we are given to concupiscence. This disease in our hearts causes us to fight against God and stimulates evil desires and appetites.

Moreover, we no longer have dominion over the earth—decay and corruption abound everywhere. The dominion of the world was taken away from us in Adam's fall into sin.[5] In our fallen state we have no right to live by the produce of this world, for it is God's world, made for God's children. Sinful persons use the earth only for the gross ends of immediate existence. We seek contentment in the pleasures of this world rather than in fellowship with God.

But good news! Restoration—restoration of individuals and restoration of the world—is promised. God redeems us in Christ to restore the original order of life. Christ restores us to the image of God lost in Adam and Eve. By faith in Christ we overcome concupiscence and turn *toward* God, not *away* from God.

Jesus shows us the living image of God. And we attempt to conform our lives to the example of the forgiving, gentle, and

generous love of God we see reflected in Jesus. We resemble
God most clearly when we do good to others, especially to the
helpless, the poor, widows, and orphans.

Our restoration also means that we live an ordered life.
Christ, the second Adam, restores us to the original order of
creation. In Jesus we see no passion that ever went spinning
out of control. So, too, must we wisely observe order, keeping
ourselves in check.

Jesus Christ also restored order to our relationship with
the world. When we are engrafted into Christ and adopted as
the children of God, we are reconstituted as lords of the world.
We have a new relationship with the environment and enjoy
God's providential care.

We take our place within God's order where God rules. We
do not belong to ourselves; we belong to God and depend on
God alone. In this pattern of order we become agents for the
restoration of order in the world. We work for the glory of God
and have fellowship with God. We serve the neighbor who is
anyone in need, far or near, even our enemies.

In the cross, God restored the whole of creation to its original glory and order. But the fulfillment of this renewal and
order through the cross progresses from day to day. Confusion
and deformity reign in the present world where evil holds
sway. But evil is being defeated—reformation and order are
taking place. The full renovation, however, will not take place
until Christ returns.

God's restoration of the world in Christ enables us to relate
properly to our earthly home. With thanksgiving to God we
use and enjoy all the blessings God showers upon us. But
when we love this present world so much that we compromise
our faith or give allegiance to the dominant evil powers, we
must repent. When we give ourselves over to concupiscence,
we must turn back to God. When we allow love for the world
to ruin our relationship with God, we must confess our sin
and hate those actions that turn us from God. Life is a gift
from God and "is still rightly to be counted among those
blessings of God which are not to be spurned."[6]

Whenever humans deny themselves and put to death concupiscence through the death of Christ, they evidence the
restoration of the Kingdom. Therefore, the conversion of the
individual is crucial; it is a sign of the restoration!

Such is the divine-human drama as we draw it from Calvin's teachings and from the scholars who know him well. In

this drama we turn toward God in faith and repentance and away from ourselves. We work for the glory of God by seeking to restore order to all creation. In Calvin's life we have the model of a Christian who participated in the reordering of society and worked toward reconciliation in the world.

The Calvin Model

As John Leith puts it, "Calvin's actual participation in the political and economic affairs of Geneva is certainly as impressive as anything he ever wrote."[7] Those who love God express their love by loving people. We cannot claim to be Christians unless we discharge our social responsibility to others by loving them. Calvin taught that we express love when we offer practical help to them. Thus the deacons in Geneva ministered to the needy in a variety of practical ways. But Calvin sought to apply God's will to all sectors of life. Investigate any sector of life in Geneva, and you will discover that Calvin was involved.

Education? Calvin passionately believed in it. He not only wanted an educated ministry for the church; he also realized the tremendous power of the humanities to enrich all of life. "How richly deserving of honour," Calvin wrote, "are the liberal arts and sciences which polish man so as to give him the dignity of true humanity."[8]

Family life? In the marriage ordinance that Calvin wrote for the Council of Geneva, he demonstrated his concern for decency and order. As a result, he worked for the basic equality between men and women.[9] His ordinance freed women from the onerous double standard of Christendom by allowing women also to divorce in cases of adultery.[10]

Economics? Take the issue of usury, lending money at interest, to illustrate Calvin's influence. Condemned in the Bible according to traditional interpretation, usury had been denounced in Christendom until his day. Calvin agreed that the Bible had forbidden the rich from devouring the poor by charging interest. But he also held that it did not forbid loans for production, a compelling need when world commerce was greatly expanding.

Politics? Calvin was accused of meddling in politics, and "meddle" he did. He appeared before the Council of Geneva so often that at times the Council must have wearied of him. But after once banishing him from Geneva, they eventually invited him back. Although Calvin had a positive regard for the state, he fought long and hard for the independence of the church from state control. He spoke against allowing men "to make laws according to their own decision concerning religion and the worship of God."[11] In his view church and state had separate spheres of responsibility. However, Calvin wanted the state to be Christian, for he believed that Christ was Lord of both church and state. Therefore, he frequently sought to influence the state to make laws which reflected the Lordship of Christ.

Education, family life, economics, politics, and social welfare—we have briefly reported Calvin's deep involvement in the life of Geneva. But perhaps we have given enough evidence to show that Calvin did not leave his faith in the sanctuary where he preached so capably, but let it walk the streets of the city. His love for God constrained him to express it by caring for people, by helping to create a just society for the good of all. In all these ways Calvin has modeled for us an enviable spirituality.

In his teachings and total involvement in Geneva, Calvin showed that living the Christian life does not separate us from the world. On the contrary, we are called into the world, for we meet God there. Engagement in social reform and renewal expresses and deepens our spirituality.

The example of Calvin still remains a model at the heart of Presbyterianism. This influence can be seen in a variety of recent Presbyterian documents, including the *Book of Order* and "A Brief Statement of Faith." The Directory for Worship of the *Book of Order* calls for doing justice according to a biblical vision. The content of justice includes:

> dealing honestly in personal and public business; exercising power for the common good; supporting people who seek the dignity, freedom, and respect that they have been denied; working for fair laws and just administration of the law; welcoming the stranger in the land; seeking to overcome the disparity between rich and poor; bearing witness against political oppression and exploitation; redressing wrongs against individuals, groups, and peoples in the church, in this nation, and in the whole world.[12]

Calvin's influence is also seen in the Form of Government of the *Book of Order,* which directs the Presbyterian Church. An early section lays a solid foundation for social responsibility by calling upon "the people of God to work for the transformation of society by seeking justice and living in obedience to the Word of God."[13] It further calls us to minister "to the needs of the poor, the sick, the lonely, and the powerless; to engage in the struggle to free people from sin, fear, oppression, hunger, and injustice; give of ourselves to the service of those who suffer; and share with Christ in the establishing of his just, peaceable, and loving rule in the world."[14] And we cannot overlook the Great Ends of the Church, among which are "the shelter, nurture, and spiritual fellowship of the children of God . . . the promotion of social righteousness; and the exhibition of the Kingdom of Heaven to the world."[15]

"A Brief Statement of Faith," the most recent Presbyterian (U.S.A.) confession, does not address the issue of the church's involvement in social issues at great length. Yet it is clear that "the Spirit gives us courage . . . to unmask idolatries in church and culture, to hear the voices of peoples long silenced, and to work with others for justice, freedom, and peace."[16]

All these references offer compelling evidence that Presbyterians have always sought to establish the Lordship of Jesus Christ in all of life. "The Lordship of Jesus Christ," says John Leith, "means that the church must be not only pure, acknowledging him as its only Lord, but also socially responsible. . . . Social action is the truest test of religion, but it is never an end in itself. It has value only as it contributes to a greater value— fellowship with God in the kingdom of God."[17] The strength of this stance toward the world has had an impact not only on those in the tradition, but those outside it. Lucien Richard, the Catholic Reformation scholar, says, "The individualistic dimensions of Calvin's spirituality did not result in the relegation of faith to the private sphere. Calvin's spirituality was a mystique of service."[18] Richard further says that Calvin's "spirituality laid the proper balance between private and public religion, between the transformation of the individual and of the community, between inwardness and outwardness . . . Calvin envisioned an integration of holiness and virtue into the political order."[19] Perhaps it is in this union of devotion to God and service for God that Reformed spirituality makes its most significant contribution to the world.

Social Ministry and Reformed Spirituality

So far we have explored the sources of the conflict within churches over social action and have reviewed the stance of

Calvin and the standards of the Presbyterian Church with respect to social engagement. We now inquire into how the church and Christians demonstrate their spirituality through efforts to work toward reconciliation in the world. Ministries of reconciliation and compassion represent different aspects of our responsibility to the neighbor, yet both are forms of Christian spirituality. In the latter, the church shows its love through care for individuals, in the former by the change of structures in society. These two aspects of neighbor love may be distinguished but not separated without doing harm to both.

What do we mean by Christian social action, which leads to reconciliation in the world? Such social action has a clear ground, the gospel, and a definite goal, the kingdom of God. It is deliberate, calculated action—action that requires planning and preparation. Moreover, it is action that requires perseverance and patience, because utopian ideals will not be immediately realized in a fallen world.

In contrast with personal ministries of compassion, social action is group action. Some groups may be small coalitions that work for social betterment in the community, as did the members of First Presbyterian in Middletown. But other issues, such as working for world peace, are so gigantic that they require the involvement of the whole denomination or the ecumenical Christian community. Social action aims to change community structures as an extension of neighbor love. A ministry of compassion may open a shelter for the homeless, but mature social action seeks to change the societal structures which create homeless people. The remedy often calls for structural changes in both community and nation. The goal of social action is the common good.

This definition suggests a "church-sized" task. Since it requires the action of the whole community, proper planning is imperative. Dieter T. Hessel, in *A Social Action Primer,* suggests five questions that provide the data for effective planning.[20] Suppose we apply these questions to the situation in Middletown. The answers to Hessel's questions express practically what we mean by corporate spirituality.

First, *What is the social problem facing us,* which we feel called by God to address; that is, what violates the justice of the kingdom of God? In Middletown it consisted of a thousand homeless people living in a town of considerable affluence.

Why does the problem exist? Or, what is the contextual origin of this condition? No single cause can be identified in Middletown but rather a complex of causes. Jobs were lost when a textile mill closed, and no community program existed to provide job training. In some cases, emotional instability led to joblessness. Racial prejudice, earning a minimum wage but not being able to afford adequate housing, drug addiction, spousal abuse, and an inability to cope worsened the situation. All these problems formed a patchwork of causes that forced persons onto the street.

What shall we do? Or, what does our obedience to Christ demand in the situation? In Middletown the deacons at First Church chose a compassionate, short-range strategy. They created a shelter for the homeless and sought funding for public toilets. A longer-term strategy, getting at one of the causes of homelessness, might be encouraging the city council to seek new industry or to offer job training for displaced workers. Still other strategies might include attacking racial prejudice so that minorities have an equal chance at available work. These approaches point to immediate and long-range solutions to the problem but do not exhaust the possibilities.

How shall we move? Or, what shape will our obedience take? In Middletown the first response had been the shelter, an action which involved using the church gymnasium and a number of volunteers from the congregation. The minister had also made a plea to the city council. Going further, the congregation could ask questions: What legislation would ensure justice for these unemployed mill workers? What educational task existed for church members? Were there official protests to make, such as resolutions, petitions, letters?

Finally, *What results are expected?* Or, how will our actions bear witness to the reign of God? Certainly the Middletown church wanted to relieve the immediate needs of people on the street, but they wanted to do more—get at the cause of homelessness. In healing the hurt of this one group, they were creating a better life for all.

In Middletown most persons could show compassion for homeless people with little internal conflict. But when people questioned the structures of the community and suggested a redistribution of power, those in control were threatened and responded angrily. Changing "the way things are" is always feared by someone and usually draws angry responses.

While the actions in Middletown stirred up deep feelings of

fear and prejudice, they are relatively mild compared to feelings related to issues like abortion, gay and lesbian concerns, burning the flag, the use of nuclear weapons, civil disobedience, and military intervention. Yet, whatever affects the way we live forces itself onto the Christian agenda for evaluation and response.

Can we profess an authentic, biblical spirituality and not be concerned with the forces that affect our lives and those of our neighbor far and near? In our tradition, social action is always motivated by love of God and neighbor—and in that order. Christians evaluate issues by standards of justice. The participants in this drama of reconciliation should be consecrated men and women who seek God's kingdom, who desire to do God's will on earth as it is in heaven.

Our conviction, grounded in the integrity of the Reformed tradition, is that Christians must work toward reconciliation in the world. Yet as we evaluate social issues, develop strategies for change, and engage in the actual tasks we must do, we do so with a deep sense of humility. We are all sinful people with corrupt hearts, so even our best virtues will be distorted by sin. Let us cast ourselves upon the mercy of God and count on divine providence to help us do God's will on earth as in heaven, using us in whatever way God may choose.

Questions for Reflection

1. What is the doctrine of the "spirituality of the church"?
2. What evidence of its influence do you find in your congregation?
3. Why must the church engage in social action?
4. How is social action the expression of the individual's and the church's true spirituality?
5. What can be done to help your congregation be more effective in seeking changes for the common good?

12

Toward Reforming
the Congregation

Peter and Mary Simpson had been members of First Presbyterian Church in Middletown for a few months over five
years. Peter had been able to get another job at a competing
engineering firm, Mary's malignancy was under control, and
the family was immersed in the life of the church and the
community. Their youngest child was nearing the end of high
school; the other was a freshman in college.

The Simpsons had come to the time in their lives when
they were able to care not only for themselves and their own
family; they felt increasingly concerned about the needs of
"the neighbor," the larger community, and the church. In his
sixth year of membership, Peter was elected an elder and was
placed on the congregational life committee.

One Friday Peter and Mary scheduled a rare evening out.
Mary arranged for reservations at one of their favorite restau-
rants. After a delightful meal, she and Peter began to recall
various experiences of the past five years, beginning with the
day they became members of the church. With delight they
recalled how their cold, impersonal world had been changed
into one in which God's presence was experienced in the
ordinary events of the day. The worship of God had become
central in their lives; they not only attended church, they
lived with an eye to pleasing and honoring God. Their sense
of God's presence had been deepened by their diligent study
of the scripture and their newfound discipline of prayer.

As they recalled these changes Mary said, "For so many
years I had been completely unaware of the significance of my
baptism. Now I know myself to be a member of Christ's Body

on earth, and my faith and hope are nurtured by the presence of Christ at the Table when I receive the sacrament."

With a chuckle Peter responded, "Mine, too! But Mary, we can't forget the challenges that have come to us—your illness, my change of jobs, the proper view and use of money. All these tests have helped us grow, but they were not easy at the time."

After Mary shared her joy in being a deacon, and the significant way First Church had gotten involved in the community life of Middletown, Peter's expression turned serious when he said, "That's true, but I've been feeling some concern about our church. Things don't seem to be like they were a few years ago."

"What do you mean?" asked Mary.

"I suppose being on the session has forced me to look at the church through different eyes. I notice that we are getting older; the budget is harder to raise; we have cut back on our outreach programs; the membership has declined for several years; Sunday school classes are being combined, and the general spirit in the church lacks energy and enthusiasm."

"What do you propose to do about the situation?" Mary asked.

"I don't know, but I'm going to express my concern at the next session meeting."

Peter did speak out and discovered that several other leaders were feeling much the same way. Three months later Peter Simpson was appointed moderator of the committee for revitalization at First Church. Perhaps Peter's concern evidences the work of the Spirit to bring reformation to the church in Middletown.

The Church Reformed, Always to Be Reformed

One principle stands at the center of the Reformed view of the church: "*Ecclesia reformata, semper reformanda*," that is, "The church reformed, *always to be reformed*." We stress the italicized translation because the church is always being reformed "according to the Word of God and the call of the Spirit."[1] The Word of God and the Spirit, the sources of the reforming impulse, empower and call the church to respond creatively to changing circumstances. Calvin's tract, *The Necessity of Reforming the Church*, clearly points out that "the restoration of the church is the work of God."[2] Nothing in life remains fixed—not the world, not the church, not the form of our spirituality. Therefore, a spiritually generative congregation will never make any form of its life permanent, but will ever be responsive to the Word of God and to the Spirit calling it to reform the practice of its faith.

The very practical question, which begs an answer, stands before us: How can Presbyterian congregations become reformed so as to be spiritually generative? To have spiritually generative congregations requires leadership from pastors and elders. With informed leadership we believe a congregation will have new vitality and a synergy between its individual and corporate dimensions. Take worship as an illustration of this synergistic effect. The individual prays and studies scripture in private, but in accord with the Reformed tradition the individual also participates in corporate worship. The dynamic synergy occurs when the individual feeds off the corporate life of worship and corporate worship receives energy from the participation of individual worshipers.

This interdependence of the individual and the community stands at the heart of Reformed spirituality and suggests a dynamic principle for the reformation of our congregational life. Thus our question: How do we develop a spiritually generative congregation? We intend to show how the church can plan and conduct its ministry so as to be conducive to spiritual growth—both its own and that of its members. These changes demonstrate the reformation principle at work.

A Generative Metaphor

In our discussion of the importance of the church in personal salvation, we offer an enticing metaphor from Calvin. He says,

> Because it is now our intention to discuss the visible church, let us learn even from the simple title "mother" how useful, indeed how necessary, it is that we should know her. For there is no other way to enter into life unless this mother conceive us in her womb, give us birth, nourish us at her breast, and lastly, unless she keep us under her care and guidance until, putting off mortal flesh, we become like the angels."[3] (See Matt. 22:30).

What a metaphor for a spiritually generative congregation: "mother." The visible church is as necessary for our spiritual birth and growth as is a mother for our physical birth and life.

Note the concrete language Calvin uses to define a spiritually generative congregation—"conceive us in her womb," "give us birth," "nourish us at her breast," "keep us under her care and guidance."

A spiritually generative congregation conceives new life in its womb—the dual action of the word of God and the Spirit of God enters human consciousness like a sperm penetrating an unfertilized egg, and this life of God is conceived in the heart. The congregation, like a womb, provides a safe and nurturing environment in which to grow. Like a mother's breasts, the church's truth and fellowship nourish the new life generated by the Spirit. With the sensitive concern of a mother, the church takes on the responsibility of caring for us through all the vicissitudes of life—sickness and health, joy and pain, success and failure, weakness and strength. We know of no metaphor so suggestive of the church's care. Mothers may be sensitive, caring, and sometimes indulgent, at other times they must use discipline. Without discipline, love easily becomes sentimentality, so the church also nurtures through the governance of its members. Like preventive medicine, discipline wards off serious illnesses.

As we offer suggestions for reforming the congregation, this metaphor of the church as mother constantly lies in the background. How can we give emphasis to the church's task of conceiving, generating, birthing, and nourishing the lives of individuals through a healthy corporate life? If we can successfully guide the church in this endeavor, maybe we can avoid that counterproductive struggle of a spiritually alive embryonic congregation existing in the womb of a sick or dying church.

Toward Reforming the Congregation

In our description of Reformed spirituality, we have pointed to the inception and context of spiritual life, to the means of grace to nourish it, and to a personal and corporate expression of spirituality in the world. If this occurs, it will require more than a theoretical description—we must suggest how leaders like Peter and Mary Simpson, Dr. Makemie, and other deacons and elders can direct this essential, corporate task. Focusing upon each aspect of Reformed spirituality, we ask a single question: How can the church's leadership plan for and guide the church in these spiritually generative tasks?

We do not wish to promise more than we can deliver, because a full answer to each question would require more than our space allows. So at best we can offer a few practical suggestions to help begin a movement toward a spiritually generative congregation. (Also see the list of Resources for Congregational Reformation in Appendix C.)

How can a congregation generate new life? Truthfulness demands the confession that spiritual generation rests with the initiative of God. Yet practical observation suggests that some contexts procreate better than others. As the "mother" metaphor suggests, some wombs conceive while others remain barren.

The answer to the question of the generation of new life within a congregation is synonymous with the evangelistic task of the church. We have written about this task elsewhere, so here our goal will be to initiate the process of self-evaluation and concrete intentionality.

Answering the following questions can turn the focus of the church in the right direction:

—Do we aim at the creation of new Christian persons?

—What approaches do we use to help individuals come to personal faith?

—Is the womb of our church conducive to conception of a Reformed spirituality?

—What contribution does each aspect of our ministry make to help persons begin an intentional Christian life?

—Do we offer ministries to persons in search of a vital faith?

—Have we in the past been effective in helping persons begin the Christian journey?

—What new decisions should we make regarding this task?

Since we cannot say everything here about making the church effective in the generation of new spiritual life, four crucial suggestions may be useful. First, let the minister and the elders become intentional in helping persons come to faith. Such new life is generated in churches which intend to do it, plan for it, and work at the task. Conversely, churches which do not intend to create new life seldom do.

In addition to deciding to make new life a goal, the leadership could plan an inquirer's class. Who are potential inquirers in your community? Personally invite them to a class to explore the meaning of Christian faith in a postmodern world. Create an atmosphere in which no question will be labeled dumb or off-limits. Persons come to a meaningful faith only when their basic questions have been answered.

Since the most effective way to generate new life is person to person sharing, ministers must train the laity to communicate their faith. We deplore rude, intrusive, manipulative "scalp hunting," as much as anyone, but one person speaking honestly with another about Christ can be positive and helpful. Select a group of interested and willing persons and spend six to eight weeks helping them identify their own faith and a few basic skills for sharing it with others. A number of good Reformed resources are available to assist in this task. (See Appendix C.)

If the congregation generates new life, it must provide vitality in preaching and worship. In the Reformed view so much depends on hearing the word of God in worship. The minister and worship leadership must remember that persons with differing needs and in varying stages of growth participate in worship. There are those who need support for their ministry, those who need comfort and encouragement, and those who need to begin an intentional Christian journey.

How do we create a spiritually generative congregation, which affirms and celebrates the presence of God? We cannot rely exclusively on the shift from an Enlightenment to a biblical worldview alone to support the awareness of God in the totality of our lives. To what other sources can we turn? First, the central time and place of spiritual renewal and celebration is the hour of formal worship in the sanctuary. Corporate worship sharpens and refines our awareness. If the liturgist and the preacher carry out their roles with a sensitivity to the holy, their manner helps the congregation become aware of God.

The way in which the church plans for and carries out its mission both models and creates a climate for spiritual awareness. The church can be operated strictly like a business, defined by goals and objectives and evaluated by the bottom line. Or the church can be like an intimate family controlled by a few matriarchs or patriarchs. Or the church may recognize itself as the Body of Christ whose mission is to re-present Christ in the world. With this realization the church, through its corporate intuition and imagination influenced by the Holy Spirit, actually performs the will of God. If the congregation functions as the Body of Christ, each ministry deepens the sense of the divine and creates within the church a culture of awareness.

The awareness of God's presence in all of life is further strengthened when the occurrences in the lives of members are publicly acknowledged and celebrated in worship. One effective means of celebration we experienced in a West Coast church came when the minister wandered through the congregation with a cordless microphone giving opportunity for members to share their lives with each other. Each offering was celebrated with a recognition of God's grace and presence. While our typical Reformed reserve would not encourage this practice every week, we believe an occasional public celebration of God's presence would inspire worshipers.

How shall we create a church with spiritually generative worship? Our statements have already underscored the centrality of worship and provided a few hints about how it should be conducted. How do we help persons prepare for and participate in worship?

Worship which intends to bring persons into the presence of God is spiritually generative. Divine presence means wonder! Awe! Decision! Transformation! It is always a gift, but our expectation and sensitivity play a role.

To offer nurture and vitality, the church must help persons learn to worship. Periodic classes in which the congregation studies the Directory for Worship and understands the various movements in worship and the use of liturgy for celebration will certainly enhance its meaning.

Congregations should build great traditions into their worship life. The annual Christmas Eve service has deep meaning for some congregations. Others stage an international Christmas pageant, or sponsor an All Saints Day memorial service to remember and celebrate the lives of those who have died during the past year. Such traditions provide substance and structure to members' lives.

How can a focus on prayer create a spiritually generative congregation? At its center, prayer means fellowship with God. Though it may take many forms, prayer receives its greatest affirmation from the example the minister and the elders set. Their regular, serious engagement in prayer provides an important model that inspires persons and leavens every other ministry of the church.

The spiritually generative congregation teaches the congregation to pray the liturgy, the order of worship for the Lord's day. The movement of the liturgy from "a call to worship" to "the benediction" can be seen as an hour-long prayer. If worshipers are no more than spectators, the corporate prayer remains only a possibility. When they engage in corporate prayer, they will likely meet God. More important, a corporate form of prayer sharpens personal prayer. We know of nothing that would more quickly transform worship than a corporate praying of the liturgy.

We recommend an annual school of prayer for each congregation. This school should be conducted by a person competent in the field who can teach both the theology and the practice of prayer. Small prayer groups, as well as more consistent personal prayer, would be a natural consequence of the school of prayer.

A spiritually generative church in prayer will provide resources for prayer—personal, family, small group, and liturgical. Churches can establish their own bookstore or a book table. A book-of-the-month on prayer, which the congregation reads together, can enrich congregational life.

Finally, a spiritually generative congregation in prayer can plan and conduct personal and group prayer retreats. We encourage persons serious about prayer to give time monthly or quarterly for personal retreats. Suggestions can be found in the last section of *A Guide to Prayer for Ministers and Other Servants.*

Large churches should have a regular retreat program that involves between twelve and twenty-four persons in each retreat. This time away should include silence, fellowship, and instruction. If a congregation does not have sufficient interest or members to conduct its own prayer retreat, it can join with other congregations at a nearby retreat center.

How shall we use the scriptures to create a spiritually generative congregation? Our examination of Reformed sources testifies repeatedly to the centrality of scripture in Reformed spirituality. Scripture contains the revelation of God; it directs us in our obedience to Christ; it mediates a consciousness of divine presence. Often the Reformed church has affirmed the scriptures of the Old and New Testaments as the authority for faith and practice. How shall the minister and those charged with Christian nurture make use of the Word of God as their authoritative norm?

In worship the scriptures must be read and expounded in the hearing of the people. "The public reading of Scripture," says the Directory for Worship, "should be clear, audible, and attentive to the meaning of the text, and should be entrusted to those prepared for such reading. Listening to the reading of Scripture requires expectation and concentration and may be aided by the availability of a printed text for the worshipers."[4] Reading scripture in unison, responsively or antiphonally, may help the congregation hear God speak through the text.

Biblical preaching addresses the mind and the heart of worshipers with relevant, carefully constructed sermons. "It is a proclamation of scripture in the conviction that through the Holy Spirit Jesus Christ is present to the gathered people, offering grace and calling for obedience."[5]

The Bible must be used as the basis of teaching and Christian nurture. The Kerygma series offers an excellent resource for adults. We also believe our children need to know the enduring stories of the faith so that their truth forms the child's picture of the world and their responsibility in it.

Many churches nurture members through small Bible study groups. These lay-led groups consist of Bible study, personal reflection, service, and prayer. In this informal, non-threatening setting, numerous persons will be challenged and enriched in their faith.

The Reformed tradition emphasizes family worship as a means of spiritual generation. "When it is possible to worship together daily, households may engage in

—table prayers, which may be accompanied by the use of Scripture and song;
—Bible reading, study, reflection, and memorization;
—singing psalms, hymns, spirituals, and other songs;
—expressions of giving and sharing."[6]

Consider these ways of stimulating Bible reading in the family: offer a guide for reading through the Bible in a three-year period; print the lectionary passages—a list for each day can be found in *A Guide to Prayer for Ministers and Other Servants, Mission Yearbook* (latest edition), and also *Daily Prayer*; and publish the text for each Sunday's sermon. (See Appendix C and Bibliography.) Encourage the use of these guides for the private reading of scripture.

However we teach or study the scripture, we need to remember our dependence upon the revealing presence of the Holy Spirit. Unless the Spirit "breathes" on scripture, its truth remains entombed. The Spirit resurrects the text and gives it life in our minds and hearts. When this divine presence through scripture enlivens persons, they bring new life into the congregation. Spiritually vital persons help to create a generative congregation.

How can a congregation use the sacraments in a spiritually generative way? Perhaps no form of ministry in the Reformed tradition holds greater potential for creating and sustaining the spirituality of the people; yet none suffers greater misunderstanding or neglect. Can the sacraments be approached differently so that they become spiritually generative?

In addition to instruction in baptism for the parents of young children, communicants classes, and adult new member classes, we encourage a clear statement of the meaning of baptism each time it is administered in the congregation and that an invitation be given to the people "to remember their baptism."

The Presbyterian Church (U.S.A.) has provided a supplemental resource for worship that contains a variety of services for the renewal of baptism: a general renewal for the congregation; a service for lapsed members; and a service of laying on of hands and prayer to commemorate a new commitment or sense of call. These public rituals of renewal hold creative possibilities for revitalizing the generative impulse of a congregation. Such liturgical services constitute the Reformed approach to personal rededication and commitment.

The Lord's Supper focuses on Christ's death for our sins and his real presence. How can the congregation celebrate the Supper in a manner that mediates these central verities? Preparation is essential. The Larger Catechism urges worshipers to prepare "by examining themselves, of their being in Christ, of their sins and wants; of the truth and measure of their knowledge, faith, repentance, love to God and the brethren, charity to all men, forgiving those that have done them wrong, of obedience; and by renewing the exercise of these graces, by serious meditation, and fervent prayer."[7]

The mediation of forgiveness depends on personal and corporate awareness of our failure to do the will of God. A vague confession of general sinfulness will have about as much meaning as the listless playing of "The Star-Spangled Banner" before a sports event. Consider asking the congregation to review their lives over the past few months to identify their sin; the week before Communion provide a copy of the Prayer of Confession so that each person may meditate on its personal application. Encourage fasting one or two meals prior to Communion—make the fast part of your tradition. Provide the congregation with scripture references to the passion of Christ—these references should be read and meditated on as preparation for receiving the sacrament.

The Supper is not only a meal of forgiveness, but also of divine presence. In whatever way we understand this mystery, the Supper represents fellowship with our Lord, who is present in us through faith as we partake of the bread and wine.

In the administration of the Supper, the minister and elders should offer it with a keen awareness of the power of the celebration for the church. The bread and wine represent God's guarantee of mercy. They are visible, tangible assurances of Christ's presence and personal forgiveness.

At the conclusion of the Supper, the minister can say to the congregation: "We are a forgiven people—believe it! We are a people who live in a consciousness of the risen Christ—believe it! Go in the sure knowledge that you are forgiven and that Christ goes with you!"

Rightly prepared for and administered, no other ministry of the church holds such generative potential!

How can self-denial help a church become spiritually generative? Our emphasis has not been on denying ourselves personal indulgences like chocolate during Lent, but on the conservation of resources and the protection of the environment, and on a consideration of justice for the poor through a simpler lifestyle. What can a congregation do to demonstrate a corporate sensitivity to those issues, and how can it support individuals who choose an alternative way of life?

The church in its image and decor can recognize that it follows the poor and lowly Jesus. This principle affects architecture, furnishings, and allocations of the budget.

The church can plan an annual Earth Day celebration to keep the stewardship of the earth in the consciousness of the people.

If persons adopt an alternative lifestyle, they will need encouragement and support. Support groups and networks will help them.

A number of projects fit into this category: recycling, the clean air movement, protest of nuclear proliferation, justice for the poor, and protest of business practices that take advantage of the weak or poor. Corporately the congregation may express itself in the form of resolutions and petitions. In all these ways, the community of faith seeks to express its personal piety in the context of social justice.

How can a congregation be spiritually generative through bearing the cross of Christ? When we recognize that often God intends the cross to teach or to chastise us, or to let us suffer persecution, we have a clue to spiritual generativity through cross bearing.

A congregation becomes spiritually generative through the pastoral care of its members who are bearing the cross. Nothing gives people a greater sense of being loved than care in crisis. Care binds them more tightly to the church. In our encouragement and support of fellow members we ought to permit persons in pain to raise the issues of God's instruction to them and of their possible chastisement. We recognize our own reluctance and probably that of others to ask these questions, but by our concern we will help those in our fellowship make their situation a means of grace.

With respect to cross bearing, the church may be called to become a sanctuary for the persecuted. Consider the example of the Presbyterian pastor in Arizona who was pushed into the sanctuary movement. He never intended to begin a refugee movement, but when persecuted brothers and sisters from Central America knocked at his door, he had no other option but to welcome the stranger. And in true biblical form, the stranger was a "bearer of divine presence," which enriched the spiritual life of the congregation.

The congregation becomes spiritually generative when it supports its own members who take daring stands for the gospel. In a sense, all these actions of the congregation express dimensions of pastoral care.

How does meditation on the future life contribute to a spiritually generative congregation? At first glance, it appears that a focus on the future life would strip the church of earthly concerns. Not so in Reformed spirituality.

The church can provide periodically a "death education" seminar either in its church school or small group ministry. When an open, accepting climate prevails, members can express their fear of old age and death. They can study biblical passages as well as the Book of Confessions to determine what our faith teaches about death. As persons study and grow together, they will discover the rich resources in our heritage for dealing with our last great enemy—death. Such a seminar might also be an ideal time to discuss funerals and to encourage members to make long-range plans for family funerals.

We believe the church should evaluate its life and ministry in the light of eternity. Practically speaking a church may conduct this evaluation by examining its budgetary expenditures. In view of God's eternal purpose, how do we evaluate our priorities as a congregation? Read each item of your budget with a picture of the poor in your community standing behind the dollar sign. Such an evaluation would encourage simplicity, holiness, and sacrifice for the congregation. Calvin reminds us that God "has also abominated excess, pride, ostentation, and vanity,"[8] and that we must regard our earthly blessings as trusts, of which we must give account. Such reflection might also alter the priorities of the General Assembly mission budget for the denomination.

How does the ministry of compassion help to create a spiritually generative congregation? One of the commendable characteristics of Reformed spirituality is the bonding of piety and compassion. There can be no Reformed spirituality without compassionate action. A deep sense of God leads to an engagement with human need; human suffering thrusts us back upon God.

Most of our congregations have some sense of responsibility for the poor and suffering. To deepen the congregation's ministry of compassion, list all the ministries of compassion presently being carried on. Include ministries conducted exclusively by the church, those shared ecumenically, and those in which individual members engage. Report to the congregation both facts and personal stories of service.

Appoint a task force to identify unmet needs in your community. Have the session order them in terms of how the church will respond.

In sermon, bulletin, newsletter, and personal appeal challenge members to share in the tasks of meeting human need. These ministries may take many forms: food, clothing, emergency aid to travelers, job training, or shelters for the homeless. One ministry of compassion will lead to the opportunity for a dozen others.

One church made a study of the state criminal justice system. The study led to the creation of a task force that developed a ministry to prisoners in a correctional institution. A literacy program with the prisoners also led to many friendships and changed the lives of both the prisoners and the church volunteers.

How can a spiritually generative congregation contribute to reconciliation in the world? In our study of Reformed spirituality we have seen how naturally spirituality flows from the personal to the corporate, from deep piety to social righteousness. How can the spiritually generative congregation be a witness to the gospel, a protest against all that obstructs justice, peace, and social righteousness? The answer to this question includes the denomination's efforts for peace and social justice. By no means will our suggestions be exhaustive.

First, bring the events of our time into the worship of the church through prayer, preaching, and announcement. These events must be viewed through the gospel, a gospel which stands above every cultural value or political ideology. Study and debate these events and participate in moral decision making with the congregation.

For example, the church must face current issues like homophobia, abortion, racism, sexism, and war. The church must struggle with the question: What are we to do in light of the gospel?

Issues of international import—shifts in the Soviet Union, the oppression of blacks in South Africa, the volatile Middle East—must be viewed from the perspective of the mission of the church. How do these changes signal the in-breaking of the kingdom of God?

When a congregation reaches a decision on an issue, it can support its view with resolutions, overtures to the General Assembly, or with protests and boycotts. The church uses these and other means to witness to the gospel.

As the church engages in reconciling acts, it must do so with a deep sense of humility. Not only is the church marred by its own sinfulness, but it, too, is a victim of cultural conditioning—all its decisions will have elements of ambiguity. Thus our witness must not be tainted with pride or dogmatism.

Reformed Spirituality: A Summary

Seminal characteristics of Reformed spirituality should be used as criteria to evaluate and redirect the congregation. These criteria applied to our practices will renew congregational life and keep us at the center of the tradition.

First and most important, Reformed spirituality is grounded in the sovereign grace of God. Our spirituality is one of response to God's initiative with us, not our seeking after God from emotional need or by spiritual formulas. All our efforts to create a spiritually generative congregation must begin with an openness to God—God's presence, power, and initiative.

Reformed spirituality also stresses human responsibility and obedience. God's sovereignty has not wiped out human freedom; rather, it frees us to live for God. In the scriptures, God has told us how to live. God has given us means of grace to strengthen us to do God's will. A spiritually generative congregation cannot avoid the hard task of obedience.

The norm for Reformed spirituality is the Word of God contained in the Old and New Testaments. The Bible teaches us all we need to know about God, and no teaching of the scriptures has been wasted. The scriptures are therefore normative for the spiritually generative congregation.

The means of grace—worship, prayer, scripture, and sacraments, as well as acts of compassion and reconciliation—have a personal and corporate dimension. For example, we worship corporately and in secret; we pray the liturgy together and make private prayers in our homes; we celebrate the sacraments as a community, but we are baptized individually and we eat and drink individually; we show corporate compassion because we are a congregation of compassionate individuals. A spiritually generative congregation will keep a balance between the individual and the corporate.

Reformed spirituality centers in a theology of the cross; it is never comfortable with the norms and values of the culture. Some aspects of Reformed spirituality seem to be world-denying, but our long history speaks otherwise. A spiritually generative congregation will therefore take the world seriously but will not ever become too cozy with the world's power, values, or forms.

Reformed spirituality maintains a creative interaction between the personal and the social. The spiritual development of individuals never has personal perfection as an end but rather personal growth and sacrificial service in society. The society provides the context of our spirituality and offers content and form for it. This interrelatedness provides a synergistic connection between personal piety and social engagement so that they are mutually energizing and transformative. A spiritually generative congregation will evaluate its life in terms of this personal/social synergy.

The church is our mother. We love her and believe that a recovery of Reformed spirituality holds great possibility for revitalizing the church. But the church must also take responsibility for reshaping her life and reevaluating her mission. The Reformed tradition of spirituality has a long and rich history and can therefore make an important contribution to the Presbyterian Church (U.S.A.) today and to the ecumenical church tomorrow.

Questions for Reflection

1. Why is the "mother" metaphor appropriate to define the church?
2. What would a spiritually generative church look like?
3. Do you consider your congregation to be spiritually generative?
4. What initial actions can your congregation take to become more generative?
5. Who must be involved if your church is to change significantly?

APPENDIXES

APPENDIX A

Lesson Plans for Group Use

Church leaders may choose either the lesson plans that follow or the alternate plans that follow Lesson 12.

LESSON 1:
To Be a Christian

Objective: To examine the meaning of living a Christian life from the Reformed perspective and to help persons have assurance they are Christian.

1. Encourage each person in the class to give regular attendance to the study. Suggest that each have a notebook in which to make outlines of the material and to prepare for class discussion. Also, encourage the use of a notebook for doing the exercises in Appendix B.

2. Let the members of the class introduce themselves and state their expectations for this class.

3. Begin the class with an overview of the four sections of the text and conclude by showing how trust in Jesus Christ as Lord and savior forms the foundation for growth in the Christian life.

4. Present the four basic aspects of being a committed Christian as outlined in chapter 1.

5. Engage the class in a discussion of how different denominations help persons make the basic Christian commitment. You may want to consider the denominations represented in the backgrounds of the class members. How do these compare and contrast with Presbyterians?

6. Elicit from the class and list on newsprint the major resistances persons have to personal commitment to Christ. Discuss how these may be overcome.

7. Assign the reading of chapter 2 and the exercises in Appendix B. Suggest they do an exercise after the study of each chapter. You may need to remind them of the exercises after each lesson.

8. If you are teaching a ninety-minute to two-hour class, you may conduct the content presentation as outlined in each lesson plan and then ask the class to divide into groups of four and to share their findings in the exercises in Appendix B.

LESSON 2:
Spirituality as Response to God's Providence

Objective: To define a worldview compatible with a vital Christian spirituality.

1. Invite the class to name the four cornerstones of an Enlightenment worldview. List these on newsprint.

2. On an overhead projector (or on newsprint) review the seminal aspects of a Reformed view of the world. Give special emphasis to Calvin's understanding of providence.

3. Ask the class to list in their notebooks the major turning points in their lives. As they look at these events through the lenses of faith, where do they discern the action of God (providence) in their lives? Have class members write short narratives describing one or two of these events.

4. In groups of two or four, depending on the size of the total group, have class members share one of these descriptions of an encounter with God. Invite one or two persons to share the narrative with the entire class.

5. Review the suggestions for deepening our awareness of God as outlined in chapter 2.

6. Ask the class to read chapter 3 and prepare answers to questions and exercises.

7. Assign one person to give a ten-minute summary of the seven points on Reformed worship at the next class.

LESSON 3:
Worship as Spiritual Formation

Objective: To enable each person to use worship as a means of grace and to deepen his or her spirituality through increased understanding of and participation in worship.

1. Invite the class to recall the most moving, enriching, or vital service of worship they ever attended. Share these experiences in groups of four.

2. Have class members identify the one element of the service that gave it significance. For example, this may include the music, the singing, or the sermon. List these items on newsprint.

3. Ask a class member to give a ten-minute report on the seven elements of Reformed worship. (Encourage the use of newsprint, slides, or an overhead projector as visual aids.)

4. Give each person a bulletin with an order of worship from the previous Sunday. Ask the class to discuss in groups of four the movements in the order and how the order embodies the Reformed tradition's view of worship. Identify the elements which you and class members have the greatest difficulty understanding.

5. Engage the class in listing on newsprint ways they can improve their preparation for each aspect of worship.

6. Write the question "How does worship relate to deepening one's spirituality?" on newsprint and ask for responses from the class.

(The Directory for Worship of the *Book of Order* and *A Study Guide for the Directory for Worship* may be helpful. Both are available from Westminster/John Knox Press, Louisville, Ky.)

LESSON 4:
Prayer as a Means of Grace

Objective: To understand the Reformed view of prayer and to enhance the practice of prayer in each person's life; to deepen his or her relationship with God.

1. Conduct a prayer survey of the class. (Make copies of the following ten questions and distribute them to the class.)

A Prayer Survey

____ T ____ F   1. I would like to improve the way I pray.

____ T ____ F   2. I have a set time for daily prayer.

____ T ____ F   3. My mind wanders when I pray.

____ T ____ F   4. I find it hard to feel God's presence when I pray.

____ T ____ F   5. I have difficulty praying regularly with my family.

____ T ____ F   6. Prayers and worship enrich my sense of God.

____ T ____ F   7. I would like to learn to pray the liturgy as a way of worship.

____ T ____ F   8. I believe God has answered prayer for me in the past.

____ T ____ F   9. My prayer discipline needs strengthening.

____ T ____ F   10. I need encouragement and accountability in my prayer life.

2. Invite members of the class to choose partners and discuss the statements of greatest concern or interest to them.

3. With newsprint or transparencies, give a brief overview of the Reformed perspective on public and private prayer.

4. Invite the class to report on their experiences with Reformed prayer. What were their problems? What were their discoveries? What resolutions will they make to enhance their prayer life?

5. As preparation for Lesson 5, assign specific persons the tasks of: (a) listening to the public reading of scripture, (b) reciting a creed, (c) meditating on a text, (d) imaginatively projecting oneself into the text, (e) paraphrasing a text, and (f) analyzing a text. Each person should be prepared to give a three- to five-minute summary of her or his findings at the next session.

LESSON 5:
Responding to Scripture as the Word of God

Objective: To learn how to listen for God through the reading of the scripture as a means of deepening one's spirituality.

1. Begin with the illustration in the text of Peter's encounter with Jim Wright. Ask the class if they know persons like Jim Wright. Discuss their responses and evaluations.

2. Invite responses to the section in chapter 5 concerning the history of how the Bible was written. Do members of the group agree or disagree with the claims made by Jim Wright?

3. Ask the class to report on experiences in which they encountered God through the study of scripture. (Be sure to emphasize that they are to share experiences, not teach a lesson. These reports were assigned to specific persons at the conclusion of Lesson 4.)

4. From the list given in chapter 5, invite the class to select the resolutions they wish to make concerning their study of scripture.

5. Ask two persons to give reports for Lesson 6, one on the scriptural basis for baptism and one on the scriptural basis for the Lord's Supper.

LESSON 6:
The Sacraments and a Vital Spirituality

Plan A

Objective: To explore ways in which the sacraments may be a means of spiritual renewal and growth.

1. Ask class members to discuss the Peter Simpson/Hal Clarke encounter. With what aspects did they identify? Give time for responses.

2. Hear the report on baptism.

3. Guide the class in a discussion of the meaning of baptism.

4. Hear the report on the Lord's Supper.

5. Guide the class in a discussion of the meaning of the Lord's Supper.

6. Invite the minister to speak to the class about his or her hopes for what might occur at each Lord's Supper and baptism.

7. Assign the class an experiment in following the Guide to Reformed Prayer in chapter 4 for one week.

Plan B

Guide the class in the following meditations.

A Guided Meditation on Baptism

1. Read Matthew 3:13–17.

2. Ask the class to become quiet, still, relaxed. Have them take six deep breaths. (1 min.)

Guide the class's meditation by providing the following images:

3. You are at the River Jordan. Visualize the crowds, hills, rivers, Jesus' arrival. (2 min.)

4. Jesus enters the water with John. John argues, "I am not worthy." He baptizes Jesus. (1 min.)

5. Jesus walks out of the water. Heaven opens. The Spirit in dove-like form falls upon Jesus. The voice: "This is my Son . . . with whom I am well pleased." (1 min.)

6. Now you are in the church's sanctuary. You kneel at the font. Listen as the minister cups water in his or her hand and lets it fall into the font, saying, "I baptize you in the name of the Father and of the Son and of the Holy Spirit." (2 min.)

7. Listen for Heaven to speak . . . "You are . . . " (3 min.)

8. Because you have been baptized into Christ you will . . . (2 min.)

9. Next, ask class members to express, in a few words, their feelings about being baptized. (3 min.)

10. Close with "Our Father, who art in heaven . . . "

11. Ask for additional personal sharing as time allows.

A Guided Meditation on the Lord's Supper

1. Read Luke 22:14–23.

2. Ask the class to be still and relax. Center their attention on the scripture passage. (2 min.)

Guide the class's meditations by providing the following images:

3. Picture the Table in the sanctuary with the elements on it. (1 min.)

4. Imagine Christ as the Host. Do not try to picture his face. See his form behind the Table as the Host. (3 min.)

5. Repeat several times his promise: "Come to me . . . and I will give you rest." (3 min.)

6. In your imagination you arise slowly and go to the Table. He breaks the bread saying, "This is my body, which is given for you. Do this in remembrance of me." (2 min.)

7. You remain at the Table. He pours the cup full and gives it to you, saying, "This cup . . . is the new covenant in my blood. Drink and be glad." (2 min.)

8. Now say what is in your heart. You have a personal audience with Christ! (3 min.)

9. Picture yourself returning to your seat. Visualize the faces who regularly share the Supper with you in church. Reflect on how Christ has given himself to them also. (2 min.)

10. Close with "Our Father . . . "

11. Ask for personal sharing.

LESSON 7:
Spirituality Requires Self-Denial

Objective: To understand self-denial as a prerequisite of love of neighbor and the expression of our Christian life.

1. Discuss Calvin's understanding of "self" in light of more contemporary views.

2. In a brief lecture, present to the class the purpose of self-denial as a transformed mind, which can give itself in love to the neighbor. Invite discussion.

3. Ask the class, in groups of four, to respond to self-denial in a global context as discussed in chapter 7.

4. Place the phrases "a supportive community" and "a new earth vision" on a page of newsprint. Invite the class to discuss these two concepts as partial solutions to living a life of self-denial.

LESSON 8:
Cross Bearing as a Form of Spirituality

Objective: To enable each person to understand the meaning of "bearing the cross" and to empower persons to bear their crosses with grace.

1. Define "cross bearing." Ask the class members to think of a cross they have been asked to bear.

2. On newsprint or transparencies, set forth the three purposes of cross bearing in lives of discipleship.

3. In groups of four, ask the class to view their cross through these three perspectives and to share their cross and its purpose in their lives.

4. Read Galatians 6:1–5. List ways we are to carry our own cross.

5. Invite the class to identify ways we may help those who have heavy crosses. (See Gal. 6:2: "Bear one another's burdens," and contrast it with Gal. 6:5: "For all must carry their own loads.")

LESSON 9:
Meditation on the Future Life

Objective: To evaluate our priorities in the light of eternity and to make appropriate shifts in lifestyle, worldview, and personal values.

Plan A

1. Define meditation. Model how to meditate on a verse of scripture. Take, for example, "The Lord is my shepherd." Repeat the verse slowly. Think about these questions: Who is the shepherd? What does he do? How does he relate to me? What will I do because he is my shepherd?

2. In a brief lecture, describe three views of the future life: Christ in us (Wallace); John's view of eternal life as a present experience (Leith and text); and ultimate fulfillment (see text).

3. Discuss three questions: (a) What purpose does meditation on the future life serve? (b) What values might change in light of this meditation? (c) What has been your experience in meditation?

Plan B

Lead the class in a meditation on Psalm 8—"The Majesty of God." This prayer springs from the heart of a person who is rightly oriented to God, a person who has realized the greatness of the Creator and the person's own finitude in the light of this vision.

1. Ask the class to listen to the words as you read Psalm 8.

2. Invite the class to repeat verse 1 in their minds for 1 minute. "O LORD, our Sovereign, how majestic is your name in all the earth!" Suggest they repeat the verse slowly, thinking about each word.

3. Read verses 2–5, pausing after each verse while the class is asked to visualize the text that was read (1 minute pause between verses).

4. Ask the class to think about their lives, their values, and their commitments and to bring these into the presence of the majestic God. (2 min.)

5. Close the meditation with the reading of Psalm 8 in unison.

6. Give a few minutes for the class to share the thoughts and feelings that arose during the meditation.

Plan C

Lead the class in a directed meditation for twenty minutes. Read the following suggestions slowly, allowing the group an opportunity to engage themselves deeply in each movement. The time allotted for each movement has been indicated in parentheses. Read the instructions slowly.

1. Sit comfortably. Relax. Take four or five deep breaths. Inhale. Exhale. Slowly. (2 min.)

2. Begin with the top of your head and think of each part of your body relaxing. Direct this relaxation from the top of the head to the tips of the toes. (Leader: you may name various body parts.) (2 min.)

3. Focus your attention on the center of your being. (1 min.)

4. A door opens at the center of your self. Enter it. Follow the pathway through a garden—to a chapel. Enter. Be seated in the chapel. Wait. Listen. (2 min.)

5. As you wait, you feel the warmth of the chapel—it begins filling with light. The light grows in its intensity until the chapel is filled, flooded with light. The light creates an awesome feeling—a sense of the Holy. You are in the presence of God. (3 min.)

6. Let yourself, your awareness remain in the "sacred light" and very slowly bring into the light the ten things you value most in your life. No conversation. No explanation. Picture one treasured thing after another in the light of the Divine Presence. (5 min.)

7. Now, let your attention return to the light of the Divine Presence—nothing else—only God. Be present to the Presence. If your mind wanders, gently pull your attention back. (3 min.)

8. Pray "The Lord's Prayer"—meditate on each phrase as you say it. Spend two full minutes contemplating the words. (2 min.)

Following the meditation, let the class share their insights or feelings about the experience.

LESSON 10:
Spirituality as Love for Neighbor

Objective: To understand compassion for the neighbor as a dimension of Reformed spirituality and to understand how we are to show neighbor love.

1. Begin class by asking members to identify their neighbors in need. Make a list of the class's response on newsprint. (Keep this list for use in Lesson 11.)

2. Review the five aspects of neighbor love discussed in the text. (You may in advance assign five persons to make a three-minute presentation of each of these.) Invite discussion on how neighbor love represents a dimension of Reformed spirituality.

3. Engage the class in listing practical ways the church may respond corporately to the neighbors in need listed previously.

4. Follow the same procedure for stating how individuals may show compassion to their neighbors.

5. Encourage the class to decide how they will share the compassion of Christ with a neighbor or group of neighbors in need.

LESSON 11:
Spirituality as Reconciliation in the World

Objective: To show that love of neighbor expresses itself in acts of reconciliation in the world and the distribution of justice to all.

1. Ask the class to describe the doctrine of the "spirituality of the church." Invite class members to state their feelings about the church's engagement in politics.

2. Evaluate the definition of social action given in chapter 11. (Or write the definition of social action on a transparency and show it to the class for discussion.)

3. Use a transparency to present the theological basis for the church's role in changing the structures of society.

4. Review the list of neighbors in need that were identified in the previous lesson. What structures of society contribute to or perpetuate their needs?

5. What changes could begin to alter the situation for them?

6. What will the class do to initiate these actions of love?

LESSON 12:
Toward Reforming the Congregation

Objective: To define a spiritually generative congregation, to evaluate the present congregation, and to adopt strategies for reforming the life of a particular congregation.

1. Invite the class to identify what a spiritually generative congregation would be like. Be specific in stating characteristics.

2. What responsibility do Christians have for the generative life of the congregation? What responsibility belongs to God?

3. Considering the various aspects of corporate spiritual life—foundation, nurture, discipline, and responsibility—where should one begin to make changes in the life of a congregation?

4. Name three strategies that the class could initiate immediately to alter the shared life of the Christian community.

5. What actions can be taken over the next six months? In a separate evaluation session, ask members of the class to reflect on their experiences and to identify:

(1) the strengths of this class

(2) the weaknesses of this class

(3) decisions they have made as a result of this class

(4) decisions they would like to be able to make

(5) a description of any new strength and energy they feel in their lives.

An Alternative Teaching Plan

Instead of these elaborate lesson plans, you could ask the class to read a chapter of the text each week and use the questions at the end of each chapter as a discussion guide. This plan may be more effective for a small group of six to eight persons.

If this plan is used, encourage the group to write their answers to the questions and/or directives in Appendix B.

Whichever way you choose to teach the material, keep a balance between an understanding of the concepts and an experience of the substance of Reformed spirituality.

For Private Study

If the text is studied individually, we encourage you to read the text, answer the questions at the end of each chapter, or use those questions for reflecting on the material. You will benefit greatly from writing your answers to the exercises in Appendix B.

APPENDIX B

Guidelines
for Spiritual
Exercises

The suggestions below follow the content offered in each chapter. Our intention has been that the reader will first understand an aspect of Reformed spirituality, and then by reflection will appropriate that insight for his or her personal life.

We believe that the following suggestions will be helpful guides for journal writing. A notebook or a bound volume or a computer may be used to record your answers for each of the questions. We encourage writing, because ideas, memories, and feelings emerge through writing in a way that simple solitary reflection does not yield.

CHAPTER 1:
To Be a Christian

1. Why do you call yourself a Christian?

2. How did you come to be a Christian?

3. Who or what has been the single most important influence in your Christian life?

4. What has been the most important truth about God in shaping your Christian life?

5. What urges to grow do you feel?

6. What anxieties, questions, or resistances do you feel in relationship to growth in your life with God?

CHAPTER 2:
Spirituality as Response to God's Providence

1. Close your eyes. Think of your life as a movie and your eyelids as a screen. Picture some of the major scenes in your life from your

earliest memory to the present as fast as you can. People who have been at the point of death say their whole life flashes before them.

2. Write a word or phrase to remind yourself of the major scenes in your life story.

3. Slowly read over these words and phrases. Feel the flow of your life. Your life has been happening; you are not in it alone. God acts in you. You are an act of God.

4. Name a few times or places in which you see the acts of God in your life.

5. How can you become more aware of God in the ordinary events of your life? (See Ben Campbell Johnson, *To Pray God's Will.* Philadelphia: Westminster Press, 1987. Note chapter 4 as a guide for seeing God in the events of the day.)

CHAPTER 3:
Worship as Spiritual Formation

1. In a short paragraph describe a time when you had a deep sense of God in a service of worship.

2. Copy the outline of worship in your notebook. Beside each movement in the order of worship, write your resolve. For example, after the call to worship write, "I will listen for God's call to me in the minister's call to worship."

3. Meditate on the movement of each aspect of worship and visualize it as a drama. Fix these moments clearly in your mind so that you can participate with understanding and enthusiasm.

CHAPTER 4:
Prayer as a Means of Grace

1. Write a short paragraph describing if, when, how, how often, and with what problems you engage in prayer.

2. Write a list of things you would like God to do for you and for others.

3. For one week, engage in a disciplined form of prayer. Use the model of Reformed prayer given in chapter 4 each morning.

After one week of praying in this manner, write your evaluation.

(a) What has been my experience in prayer this week?

(b) With which movements of prayer did I struggle most?

(c) What problems have I encountered in prayer?

(d) What benefits have I received through a disciplined approach to prayer?

(e) How would you compare personal with corporate prayer?

(f) How can you make your life a prayer?

CHAPTER 5:
Responding to Scripture as the Word of God

In this exercise we invite you to listen to God's word in three modes.

1. In Jesus' farewell address to his disciples he said, "Those who love me will keep my word, and my Father will love them, and we will come to them and make our home with them" (John 14:23).

    (a) What do these words mean?

    (b) What did these words mean to the original hearers, the disciples?

    (c) What do they mean to you today?

2. Write a paraphrase of the verse cited above.

3. Engage in an imaginative participation in scripture.

    (a) Read Mark 1:40–46.

    (b) Imagine that you are an outside observer sitting on a hill overlooking the encounter of Jesus with the leper. Write a full first-person description of what you see.

    (c) After you have written the description, think of the question which comes most naturally to you to ask Jesus. Write your question and imagine Jesus' answer to it. Let this begin a written dialogue between you and Christ.

    (d) Read over what you have written. Write a prayer expressing your feelings after this exercise.

CHAPTER 6:
The Sacraments and a Vital Spirituality

1. Write a letter to those persons responsible for your baptism in which you express your gratitude.

2. Write a prayer thanking God for your baptism.

3. Close your eyes. Picture Christ at the Communion table in your church inviting you and the congregation to sit and eat with him. After three or four minutes, describe the feelings and thoughts that came to you.

4. If the Lord's Supper is a meal of presence and forgiveness, write a few resolves about how you will participate in the next Communion.

5. After you partake of the sacrament, how can your life demonstrate that you have communed with the risen Christ?

CHAPTER 7:
Spirituality Requires Self-Denial

1. Think of lust and concupiscence as an addiction. To what are you addicted? That is, what competes with God for your loyalty?

2. If self-denial is to help us get control of ourself and to triumph over our addictions, what decisions must you make?

3. What extravagance or indulgence do you need to combat with self-denial?

4. What personal discipline can you adopt that will show your concern for pollution, consumption, or solidarity with the oppressed peoples of the world?

CHAPTER 8:
Cross Bearing as a Form of Spirituality

1. Describe one cross you have had to bear. What is it? When did it come to you? How did you feel about it? What changes has it worked in your life?

2. Is this cross to teach you? Chasten you? Is it a persecution? Give reasons for your answer. Is it still a mystery?

3. Have you willingly accepted this cross?

4. Have you asked God to bring good out of your suffering?

5. Describe how the cross has achieved its purpose in bringing you closer to God. (Or perhaps, has distanced you from God.)

6. Meditate on the old hymn:

> Must Jesus bear the cross alone and
>   all the world go free?
> No, there's a cross for everyone and
>   there is a cross for me.

7. Write your reflections.

CHAPTER 9:
Meditation on the Future Life

1. Paraphrase and personalize Matthew 6:19–21: "Do not store up for yourselves treasures on earth, where moth and rust consume and where thieves break in and steal; but store up for yourselves treasures in heaven, where neither moth nor rust consumes and where thieves do not break in and steal. For where your treasure is, there your heart will be also."

2. List ten things you value most.

3. Use the following questions as a way of reflecting upon your values and priorities.

    (a) Which have lasting significance?

    (b) Which involve other persons?

    (c) With which are you most pleased?

    (d) Which have biblical legitimacy?

    (e) Which are self-centered and self-serving?

    (f) Which demand something from you?

    (g) Which promise to reward you?

    (h) Which are corporate in nature with respect to freedom, justice, peace, etc.?

    (i) Which contribute to the world's problems?

    (j) Which seem consistent with the spirit of Jesus?

4. Review these values in the light of eternity, eternal life, or the future life. Are there changes you wish to make?

5. What is the relationship between your values and your spiritual life?

CHAPTER 10:
Spirituality as Love for Neighbor

1. In a short paragraph, describe spirituality as love of God and love of neighbor.

2. Who are neighbors in need of love in your personal life?

3. Who are neighbors in need of love in your community?

4. Who are neighbors in the larger world who need your love?

5. Name one way you can love God by loving these neighbors.

6. What changes in your present lifestyle would love of neighbor require?

CHAPTER 11:
Spirituality as Reconciliation in the World

1. What resistance have you felt to social action to correct evil in society?

2. Where did this resistance originate? Who has been a primal influence in your view?

3. What issues do you see in your community that need to be addressed?

4. What can you do to form or participate in a concerned group in the church to address these issues?

5. In a short paragraph, state how these actions would be an expression of your own spirituality.

CHAPTER 12:
Toward Reforming the Congregation

1. Is your congregation spiritually generative? Give reasons for your answer.

2. Who in your congregation could assist in making it a more spiritually generative community?

3. Review the numerous suggestions for creating a spiritually generative congregation. Is there one directive you could initiate?

4. Write a prayer for your congregation to become more spiritually generative.

5. Reflect on these exercises and the content of this study. Also write a description of the foundation of the spiritual life, the means of grace, the challenges and the responsibilities of a Christian in the Reformed tradition.

APPENDIX C

Resources
for Congregational
Reformation

The numbers correspond with the questions posed in chapter 12.
1. Richard Stoll Armstrong. *Faithful Witnesses.* Philadelphia: Geneva Press, 1987.

   Joe Donaho. *Good News Travels Faster.* Atlanta: CTS Press, 1990.

   Ben Campbell Johnson. *An Evangelism Primer.* Atlanta: John Knox Press, 1983.

   ———. *Friendmaker for God.* Atlanta: CTS Press, 1986.

   Robert H. Ramey, Jr. *The Minister's Role in Evangelism.* Atlanta: CTS Press, 1985.

2. & 3. C. Benton Kline, Jr. *A Study Guide for the Directory for Worship.* Louisville: Presbyterian Publishing House, 1990.

   The Service for the Lord's Day. Supplemental Liturgical Resource 1. Philadelphia: Westminster Press, 1984.

   Ben Campbell Johnson. *To Will God's Will,* chapter 5. Philadelphia: Westminster Press, 1987.

4. Reuben P. Job and Norman Shawchuck. *A Guide to Prayer for Ministers and Other Servants.* Nashville: The Upper Room, 1983.

   Daily Prayer. Supplemental Liturgical Resource 5. Philadelphia: Westminster Press, 1987.

   Martha Jane Petersen. *Retreat Guide.* Atlanta: CTS Press, 1991.

5. *Holy Baptism and Services for the Renewal of Baptism.* Supplemental Liturgical Resource 2. Philadelphia: Westminster Press, 1985.

Notes

Preface

1. John A. Mackay, *The Presbyterian Way of Life* (Englewood Cliffs, N.J.: Prentice-Hall, 1960), p. 9.

Chapter 1: To Be a Christian

1. Adapted from *Holy Baptism and Services for the Renewal of Baptism*, Supplemental Liturgical Resource 5 (Philadelphia: Westminster Press, 1985), pp. 28–29, 73–74.

2. David Steele, "Presbyterian Language," *Presbyterian Outlook,* January 15, 1990.

3. Theology and Worship Ministry Unit, Presbyterian Church (U.S.A.), *Growing in the Life of Christian Faith.* Report to the 201st General Assembly (1989), (Louisville, Ky., 1989), p. 1.

4. *Ibid.*

5. A Declaration of Faith (1977), *Our Confessional Heritage* (Atlanta: Presbyterian Church in the United States, 1978).

6. John H. Leith, *John Calvin's Doctrine of the Christian Life,* p. 17.

7. *Ibid.,* p. 45.

8. *Growing in the Life of Christian Faith,* p. 6.

9. The Westminster Confession of Faith, Presbyterian Church (U.S.A.), *Book of Confessions,* 6.079. (Cited hereafter as *Book of Confessions.*)

10. John Calvin, *Institutes of the Christian Religion,* McNeill-Battles translation, 3.2.7, p. 551; italics added.

11. *Growing in the Life of Christian Faith,* p. 10.

12. Leith, *John Calvin's Doctrine,* p. 46; *Corpus Reformatorum: Joannis Calvini Opera Quae Supersunt Omnia,* ed. W. Baum, E.

Cunitz, and E. Reuss (Brunswick: C. A. Schwetschke & Sons, 1863–1897), vol. 52, col. 104; vol. 26, col. 128. This work is cited hereafter as *CR,* followed by volume and column numbers (as CR 52:104). (References to *CO* refer to *Calvini Opera,* volumes 29–87 of *Corpus Reformatorum.*)

13. Ronald S. Wallace, *Calvin's Doctrine of the Christian Life,* p. 321.

14. See Presbyterian Church (U.S.A.), *Book of Order,* G-6.0102 and G-5.0102. (Cited hereafter as *Book of Order.*)

15. Shirley C. Guthrie, Jr., *Christian Doctrine,* p. 356.

16. Cited by Kenneth A. Briggs, *Progressions: A Lilly Endowment Occasional Report,* vol. 2, no. 1, January 1990, p. 7.

Chapter 2: Spirituality as Response to God's Providence

1. Quoted in Diogenes Allen, *Christian Belief in a Postmodern World,* p. 2.

2. *Ibid.*

3. *Ibid.,* pp. 4, 5.

4. Calvin, *Institutes* 1.5.3, p. 54.

5. *Ibid.,* 1.5.5, p. 57.

6. *Ibid.,* 1.16.1, p. 197.

7. *Ibid.,* 1.16.4, p. 203.

8. *Ibid.,* 1.16.7, p. 206.

9. *Ibid.,* 1.16.8, p. 208.

10. Shirley C. Guthrie, Jr., *Christian Doctrine,* p. 174.

11. See Jürgen Moltmann, *The Crucified God* (London: SCM Press, 1974).

12. For a discussion of the conversion and call of John Calvin, see Ronald S. Wallace, *Calvin, Geneva, and the Reformation.*

13. See the further discussion of cross bearing and God's providence in chapter 8.

Chapter 3: Worship as Spiritual Formation

1. Calvin, *Institutes* 2.8.16, p. 382.

2. *Growing in the Life of the Christian Faith,* p. 41.

3. John H. Leith, *An Introduction to the Reformed Tradition,* p. 80.

4. C. Benton Kline, Jr., "Individual Prayer and Corporate Prayer," *Reformed Liturgy and Music* 21, no. 4 (Fall 1987): 202–204.

5. John Calvin, *Opera Selecta* (ed. P. Barth and W. Niesel; Mu-

nich, Chr. Kaiser, 1926), 2:15; quoted in John H. Leith, *Introduction to the Reformed Tradition,* p. 167.

6. See Hughes Oliphant Old, *Worship,* p. 7.

7. Adapted from Directory for Worship, *Book of Order,* W-3.3000-3.3702.

Chapter 4: Prayer as a Means of Grace

1. Karl Barth, *Prayer,* p. 33.

2. Presbyterian Church (U.S.A.), Directory for Worship, *Book of Order,* W-2.1001.

3. Barth, *Prayer,* p. 33.

4. Karl Barth, *Church Dogmatics* III/4, p. 109.

5. Barth, *Prayer,* p. 33.

6. The Larger Catechism, *Book of Confessions,* 7.288.

7. Calvin, *Institutes* 3.20.17, p. 874.

8. George S. Heyer, Jr., "Prayer in the Reformed Tradition," *Bulletin* (Austin Presbyterian Theological Seminary), 101, no. 4 (October 1985): 40.

9. See Ronald Wallace, *Calvin's Doctrine of the Christian Life,* p. 286.

10. Calvin, *Institutes* 3.20.5, p. 855.

11. Wallace, *Calvin's Doctrine,* p. 276.

12. Calvin, *Institutes* 3.20.48, p. 916.

13. See Albert C. Winn, *A Christian Primer.*

14. The Larger Catechism, *Book of Confessions,* 7.290.

15. Calvin, *Institutes* 3.20.28, p. 888.

16. George S. Heyer, Jr., "Prayer in the Reformed Tradition," p. 41.

Chapter 5: Responding to Scripture as the Word of God

1. Calvin, *Institutes* 3.12.3, p. 924.

2. "A Brief Statement of Faith: Presbyterian Church (U.S.A.)" (Louisville, Ky.: Office of the General Assembly, 1990), lines 58-60.

3. John Calvin, *CR* 40:61-62, quoted in John H. Leith, *John Calvin's Doctrine of the Christian Life,* p. 63.

4. See Leith, *John Calvin's Doctrine,* pp. 63ff.

5. The Larger Catechism, *Book of Confessions,* 7.265.

6. Directory for Worship, *Book of Order,* W-2.2010.

7. The Westminster Confession of Faith, *Book of Confessions,* 6.117.

8. Directory for Worship, *Book of Order,* W-5.3001.

9. Quoted in Don Postema, *Space for God: The Study and Practice of Prayer and Spirituality,* pp. 124–125.

10. Directory for Worship, *Book of Order,* W-5.3003.

11. The Confession of 1967, *Book of Confessions,* 9.30.

12. John Calvin, *CR* 9:823, as quoted in John Leith, *John Calvin's Doctrine of the Christian Life,* p. 56.

Chapter 6: The Sacraments and a Vital Spirituality

1. Calvin, *Institutes* 4.14.1, p. 1276.

2. *Ibid.,* 4.14.3, p. 1278.

3. The Heidelberg Catechism, *Book of Confessions,* 4.066.

4. See The Westminster Confession of Faith, *Book of Confessions,* 31.5.

5. Catherine Gunsalus Gonzales, "Baptism and Communion Seal God's Promises," *Presbyterian Survey,* July/August 1982, p. 29.

6. See The Larger Catechism, *Book of Confessions,* 7.286.

7. The Heidelberg Catechism, *Book of Confessions,* 4.066.

8. Catherine Gunsalus Gonzales, *A Theology of the Lord's Supper,* p. 13.

9. Calvin, *Institutes* 4.15.3, p. 1305.

10. *Ibid.,* 4.15.1, p. 1303.

11. Directory for Worship, *Book of Order,* W-2.3006.

12. Laurence Stookey, *Baptism: Christ's Act in the Church* (Nashville: Abingdon Press, 1982), pp. 75, 127.

13. Calvin, *Institutes* 4.14.17, p. 1292. Italics added.

14. Calvin, *Institutes* 4.17.42, p. 1420.

15. Robert M. Shelton, "A Theology of the Lord's Supper from the Perspective of the Reformed Tradition," *Reformed Liturgy and Music* 26, no. 1 (Winter 1982): 10.

16. Calvin, *Institutes* 4.17.11, p. 1372.

17. The Westminster Confession of Faith, *Book of Confessions,* 6.617.

18. Shelton, "A Theology of the Lord's Supper," p. 6.

19. *Ibid.,* p. 6.

20. *Ibid.,* p. 5.

21. Directory for Worship, *Book of Order,* W-2.4010.

22. The Larger Catechism, *Book of Confessions,* 7.278. Italics added.

23. "Blest Be the Tie That Binds," *The Presbyterian Hymnal* (Louisville: Westminster/John Knox Press, 1990), no. 438.

Chapter 7: Spirituality Requires Self-Denial

1. Ronald S. Wallace, *Calvin's Doctrine of the Christian Life*, p. 94.
2. Calvin, *Institutes* 3.7.1, p. 689.
3. Wallace, *Calvin's Doctrine*, p. 53.
4. See *Ibid.*, p. 54.
5. *Ibid.*, p. 64.
6. *Ibid.*, p. 66.
7. *Ibid.*, p. 58.
8. *Ibid.*, p. 59.
9. *Ibid.*, p. 61.
10. Calvin's *Institutes* 3.7.8, p. 698.
11. *Ibid.*, 3.7.1, p. 690.
12. *Ibid.*
13. *Ibid.*, 3.7.4–3.7.8, pp. 693–699.
14. *Ibid.*, 3.7.5, p. 695.
15. *Ibid.*, 3.7.6, p. 696.
16. Wallace, *Calvin's Doctrine*, p. 64.
17. The Simple Living Collective, *Taking Charge* (New York: Bantam Books, 1977), pp. 334–335.
18. Calvin, *Institutes* 3.10.15, p. 723.

Chapter 8: Cross Bearing as a Form of Spirituality

1. Karl Barth, *Church Dogmatics* IV/2, p. 599.
2. *Ibid.*, p. 611.
3. Calvin, *Institutes* 1.16.4, pp. 201–202.
4. These various aspects of God's will have been adapted from Leslie Weatherhead's categories in *Salute to a Sufferer* (Nashville: Abingdon Press, 1963).
5. John H. Leith, *John Calvin's Doctrine of the Christian Life*, p. 78.
6. Calvin, *Institutes* 3.8.2, p. 703.
7. *Ibid.*, 3.8.3, p. 704.
8. *Ibid.*
9. *Ibid.*, 3.8.6, p. 706.
10. Leith, *John Calvin's Doctrine*, p. 79.
11. Barth, *Church Dogmatics* IV/2, p. 613.
12. Leith, *John Calvin's Doctrine*, p. 79.
13. Calvin, *Institutes* 3.8.5, p. 705.
14. See Ronald S. Wallace, *Calvin's Doctrine of the Christian Life*, pp. 65, 78.

Chapter 9: Meditation on the Future Life

1. Calvin, *Institutes* 3.9.1, p. 712.
2. *Ibid.,* 3.9.5, p. 717.
3. Ronald S. Wallace, *Calvin's Doctrine of the Christian Life,* p. 87.
4. *Ibid.,* p. 88.
5. *Ibid.*
6. John H. Leith, *John Calvin's Doctrine of the Christian Life,* p. 80.
7. Wallace, *Calvin's Doctrine,* pp. 90–91.
8. Calvin, *Institutes* 3.9.5, p. 718.

Chapter 10: Spirituality as Love for Neighbor

1. John H. Leith, *John Calvin's Doctrine of the Christian Life,* p. 189.
2. See Jeannine E. Olson, *Calvin and Social Welfare.*
3. John Calvin, *CR* 45:612, quoted in John H. Leith, *John Calvin's Doctrine of the Christian Life,* p. 188.
4. Calvin, *Institutes* 3.7.5, p. 695.
5. Paul Geren, *Burma Diary* (New York: Harper & Brothers, 1943, pp. 51–52); quoted in Rachel Henderlite, *A Call to Faith* (Richmond: John Knox Press, 1955), pp. 185–186.
6. Calvin, *Institutes* 3.7.6, p. 696.
7. John Calvin, Sermon on Gal. 6:9–11, *CO* 51:105, quoted in Ronald S. Wallace, *Calvin's Doctrine,* p. 150.
8. John Calvin, Sermon on 1 Cor. 11:11–16, *CO* 49:739, quoted in Wallace, *Calvin's Doctrine,* p. 154.
9. John Calvin, Sermon on Deut. 2:1–7, *CO* 26:9, quoted in Wallace, *Calvin's Doctrine,* p. 152.

Chapter 11: Spirituality as Reconciliation in the World

1. Ernest Trice Thompson, *The Spirituality of the Church,* p. 21.
2. James Henley Thornwell, *The Collected Writings of James Henley Thornwell,* eds. John B. Adger and John L. Girardeau (pp. 500–501), quoted in Ernest Trice Thompson, *The Spirituality of the Church,* p. 25.
3. Presbyterian Church (U.S.A.), "The Confession of 1967," 9.06.
4. See Ronald S. Wallace, *Calvin's Doctrine of the Christian Life,* pp. 104, 105.
5. *Ibid.,* p. 131.

6. Calvin, *Institutes,* 3.9.3, p. 714.

7. John H. Leith, *John Calvin's Doctrine of the Christian Life,* p. 197.

8. John Calvin, commentary on 1 Cor. 1:20, quoted in Ronald S. Wallace, *Calvin, Geneva, and the Reformation,* p. 101.

9. See W. Fred Graham, *The Constructive Revolutionary: John Calvin and His Socio-Economic Impact,* pp. 57–58.

10. *Ibid.,* p. 153.

11. Calvin, *Institutes* 4.20.3, p. 1215.

12. Directory for Worship, *Book of Order,* W-2.0200; W-7.4002.

13. Form of Government, *Book of Order,* G-2.0500.

14. *Ibid.,* G-3.0300.

15. *Ibid.,* G-1.0200.

16. "A Brief Statement of Belief: Presbyterian Church (U.S.A.)" (Louisville, Ky.: Office of the General Assembly, 1990), lines 66, 69–71.

17. Leith, *John Calvin's Doctrine,* p. 211.

18. Lucien Richard, *The Spirituality of John Calvin,* p. 177.

19. *Ibid.,* p. 179.

20. Dieter T. Hessel, *A Social Action Primer,* pp. 68–88.

Chapter 12: Toward Reforming the Congregation

1. Directory for Worship, *Book of Order,* W-2.0200.

2. John H. Leith, *John Calvin's Doctrine of the Christian Life,* p. 168.

3. Calvin, *Institutes* 4.1.4, p. 1016.

4. Directory for Worship, *Book of Order,* W-2.2006.

5. *Ibid.,* W-2.2007.

6. *Ibid.,* W-5.7001.

7. The Larger Catechism, *Book of Confessions,* 7.282.

8. Calvin, *Institutes* 3.10.5, p. 723.

Bibliography

Allen, Diogenes. *Christian Belief in a Postmodern World.* Louisville, Ky.: Westminster/John Knox Press, 1989.

Alston, Wallace M., Jr. *The Church.* Guides to the Reformed Tradition. Atlanta: John Knox Press, 1984.

Barth, Karl. *Church Dogmatics.* Edinburgh: T. & T. Clark, 1936–1969.

———. *Prayer.* 2nd ed. Ed. Don E. Saliers. Philadelphia: Westminster Press, 1985.

Calvin, John. *Institutes of the Christian Religion.* Ed. John T. McNeill; trans. Ford Lewis Battles. 2 vols. Philadelphia: Westminster Press, 1960.

Gonzales, Catherine Gunsalus. *A Theology of the Lord's Supper.* Atlanta: General Assembly Mission Board, Presbyterian Church in the United States, 1981.

Graham, W. Fred. *The Constructive Revolutionary: John Calvin and His Socio-Economic Impact.* Atlanta: John Knox Press, 1971.

Guthrie, Shirley C., Jr. *Christian Doctrine.* Richmond: CLC Press, 1968.

———. *Diversity in Faith—Unity in Christ.* Philadelphia: Westminster Press, 1986.

Hessel, Dieter T. *A Social Action Primer.* Philadelphia: Westminster Press, 1972.

———. *Social Ministry.* Philadelphia: Westminster Press, 1982.

Johnson, Ben Campbell. *Discerning God's Will.* Louisville, Ky.: Westminster/John Knox Press, 1990.

———. *An Evangelism Primer.* Atlanta: John Knox Press, 1983.

———. *To Pray God's Will: Continuing the Journey.* Philadelphia: Westminster Press, 1987.

————. *To Will God's Will: Beginning the Journey.* Philadelphia: Westminster Press, 1987.

Kline, C. Benton, Jr. *A Study Guide for the Directory for Worship.* Louisville, Ky.: Presbyterian Publishing House, 1990.

Leith, John H. *Introduction to the Reformed Tradition.* Atlanta: John Knox Press, 1977.

————. *John Calvin's Doctrine of the Christian Life.* Louisville, Ky.: Westminster/John Knox Press, 1989.

The Office of Worship for the Presbyterian Church (U.S.A.) and the Cumberland Presbyterian Church. *Daily Prayer.* Supplemental Liturgical Resource 5. Philadelphia: Westminster Press, 1987.

————. *Holy Baptism and Services for the Renewal of Baptism.* Supplemental Liturgical Resource 2. Philadelphia: Westminster Press, 1985.

————. *The Service for the Lord's Day.* Supplemental Liturgical Resource 1. Philadelphia: Westminster Press, 1984.

Old, Hughes Oliphant. *Worship.* Guide to the Reformed Tradition. Atlanta: John Knox Press, 1984.

Olson, Jeannine E. *Calvin and Social Welfare.* Selinsgrove, Pa.: Susquehanna University Press, 1989.

Postema, Donald H. *Space for God: The Study and Practice of Prayer and Spirituality.* Grand Rapids: Bible Way, 1983.

Presbyterian Church (U.S.A.). *The Constitution of the Presbyterian Church (U.S.A.), Part I: Book of Confessions.* Louisville, Ky.: Office of the General Assembly, 1990.

Presbyterian Church (U.S.A.). *The Constitution of the Presbyterian Church (U.S.A.), Part II: Book of Order.* Louisville, Ky.: Office of the General Assembly, 1990.

Ramey, Robert H., Jr. *The Minister's Role in Evangelism.* Decatur, Ga.: CTS Press, 1985.

Richard, Lucien. *The Spirituality of John Calvin.* Atlanta: John Knox Press, 1974.

Theology and Worship Ministry Unit, Presbyterian Church (U.S.A.), *Growing in the Life of Christian Faith.* Louisville, Ky.: 1989. (Also printed in *Minutes of the 201st General Assembly (1989) of the Presbyterian Church (U.S.A.), Part I: Journal,* pp. 467–487.)

Thompson, Ernest Trice. *The Spirituality of the Church.* Richmond: John Knox Press, 1961.

Wallace, Ronald S. *Calvin, Geneva, and the Reformation.* Grand Rapids: Baker Book House, 1988.

———. *Calvin's Doctrine of the Christian Life.* Tyler, Tex.: Geneva Divinity School Press, 1982.

Winn, Albert C. *A Christian Primer.* Louisville, Ky.: Westminster/ John Knox Press, 1990.